# EMOTIONS AS RESOURCES

*Pastoral Renewal Books are published by Servant Books in cooperation with the Center for Pastoral Renewal.*

# Emotions as Resources

*A Biblical and Pastoral Perspective*

Bert Ghezzi
Mark Kinzer

 A Pastoral Renewal Book

SERVANT BOOKS
Ann Arbor, Michigan

Published by Servant Books
        P.O. Box 8617
        Ann Arbor, Michigan 48107

Book and jacket design by John B. Leidy
Cover photos: top left and right, Stock Boston; lower left,
John Leidy; lower right, Evan Johnson, Jeroboam, Inc.


Printed in the United States of America
ISBN 0-89283-158-8

# Contents

*Acknowledgments* / vi

Introduction / 1
1. A Biblical Perspective / 3
2. A Pastoral Strategy / 15
3. Desiring What God Desires / 33
4. True and False Humility / 51
5. Not Guilty! / 63
6. What Should Christians Teach about Anger? / 79
7. The Gift of Fear / 91

*Notes* / 107
*Suggested Reading* / 109

# Acknowledgments

THIS BOOK was prepared under the auspices of the Center for Pastoral Renewal, an interdenominational organization devoted to spiritual and pastoral renewal. Among other concerns, the Center is eager to help Christian leaders provide practical teaching about basic elements of Christian living. The material in this book has appeared in slightly different form in *Pastoral Renewal*.

# Introduction

OUR EMOTIONS are resources for Christian living which should be integrated into our personalities as God-given and inherently valuable qualities, like the intellect and the will. Yet today, emotions often seem to become detached from the rest of our personalities, taking on a life of their own. For many Christians, emotions are liabilities, not resources. They have become fearsome enemies or dictatorial masters. People analyze, repress, dwell on, indulge, and worry about their emotions.

We believe that emotions should be our servants, and that God intends to transform people so that their emotions instinctively support them in righteous living. Our aim in this book is to help pastors of churches, leaders of Christian groups, and other Christians with pastoral responsibilities to develop a strategy that will enable Christians to get their emotions working the way they should. While we address our remarks primarily to those with pastoral responsibility, the biblical approach to the emotions presented here should be useful to any Christian. We would especially mention parents, who of course *do* have pastoral responsibility, as well as anyone who is seriously concerned about growing to maturity in the Christian life.

This book's perspective on emotions is rooted in a careful consideration of scripture and in many years of pastoral experience in a variety of Christian groups. Our study of the Bible convinced us that scripture contains a teaching on emotional health which Christians today must recover. While the Bible does not discuss emotions in exhaustive detail, it does contain instruction about how emotions should work in the lives of those who follow the Lord Jesus. It gives numerous examples of men and women whose emotions support them in righteousness, examples which include Jesus himself.

This specific approach to emotions was developed and tested in the lives of thousands of Christians in churches, prayer groups, communities, and other kinds of Christian groups over the past twenty years. The authors developed their pastoral strategy in collaboration with a sizeable group of other Christian leaders who are associated with them in pastoral care. In other words, the teaching in this book does not represent an untested theory or some kind of an ideal yet to be attained. It does work. It is a strategy that has proven itself to be a useful pastoral tool.

Our approach is not intended for Christians with serious emotional problems. Quite often, those with severe disturbances require medical care and competent Christian psychological counseling. Our primary aim is to help those who are in good mental health—that vast majority of us whose emotional problems fall somewhere short of being called "serious."

This book was written by both of us but each has had primary responsibility for certain chapters. Bert Ghezzi wrote those on pastoral strategy, anger, and fear. Mark Kinzer wrote the chapters on the biblical perspective, humility, desires, and guilt. Chapter 1 sets forth the scriptural teaching on emotions in some detail. Chapter 2 develops the pastoral strategy for the emotions as resources. Succeeding chapters study specific emotions as illustrations of how the strategy works. We do not intend to provide exhaustive treatment of all the emotions. Rather, we intend to take a close look at desires, anger, fear, humility, and guilt in the hope that by so doing we will arrive at an understanding of how emotions can serve rather than hinder or rule us.

People today tend to think of such emotions as problems. Indeed they can be problems, but in many cases they are problems that can be overcome. Above all, we believe that the emotions—properly understood, channeled, and pastored— can be valuable resources in the Christian life.

# ONE

# A Biblical Perspective

IMAGINE YOURSELF sitting in your favorite lounge chair on a cold winter evening, reading the Bible, when you hear a knock on the front door. Opening the door, you behold a small, bearded man clothed in greyish robes. He explains that he is a Judaean merchant from the eighth century B.C., and he needs a place to stay while in town. You have plenty of space in your home, so you welcome this curious visitor as a guest.

After living with him for a few days, you begin to notice many odd features about this man. Some of these features clearly stem from his unusual personal habits, but others seem to be rooted more deeply in the makeup of his personality. He seems less introspective than other men you have known, less moody, less concerned with how he or other people are feeling. At the same time, he is gracious and considerate, and sometimes embarrassingly uninhibited about expressing respect, affection, and occasionally anger.

Unfortunately, none of us will ever have the opportunity to meet an ancient Israelite or a first-century Christian (and even if we did, few of us would be able to converse comfortably with them in their own languages). However, if such an encounter were possible, we would certainly notice differences between the psychology of a biblical man and the psychology of a modern man. In particular, we would notice differences in thinking and talking about emotions and in handling emotions in daily life.

People in modern society monitor their feelings closely—Am

3

I angry, happy, or sad?—and make emotional states the basis of their personal relationships. People in biblical societies took a very different approach. They were more interested in the nature of their situation and the behavior appropriate to that situation. They had norms for handling personal relationships and the circumstances of daily life, and they allowed their emotions to support them and serve them in following these norms.

This psychological difference between biblical and twentieth-century people can often lead to misunderstandings of scripture. When men or women today read scripture and come upon such words as "peace," "love," "joy," "anger," and "fear," they naturally interpret these words as referring largely to subjective emotional states. The biblical injunctions to love God and neighbor, rejoice in all circumstances, and fear secular rulers thus become commands to maintain a particular set of internal states. To interpret the scripture in this way is to misunderstand much of what it is trying to say.

## Peace and Love: Feelings?

There are two areas of misunderstanding. The first involves biblical words which are often interpreted as emotions but refer instead to objective conditions or actions. For example, in scripture the word "peace" (Hebrew, *shalom*; Greek, *eirene*) means the fullness of blessing or well-being: health, prosperity, salvation (Gn 43:27; Ps 37:11; Lk 1:79; Lk 19:42), a loving and well-ordered set of personal relationships (Gn 26:29; Acts 15:33; Rom 5:1; 1 Cor 14:33; Col 3:15), and security and freedom from conflict or danger (Ps 55:18; Lk 11:21; Lk 14:32). "Peace" is both the description of and the result of a right relationship with God. The tendency of the modern reader is to think of this rich biblical word as primarily describing an internal sense of tranquility, quietude, and freedom from anxiety or psychological conflict. Though such feelings will usually accompany the objective condition of peace, they are not central to the meaning of *shalom* or *eirene*.

Similarly, the main word for love in the New Testament (*agape*) does not refer to an emotion. *Agape* is a way of acting, a way of relating to other people and to God. It involves service and personal care, and is demonstrated perfectly in Jesus' offering of his life upon the cross (Jn 15:12-13; Rom 5:6-8; 1 Jn 3:16; 1 Jn 4:7-12). A modern reader will often understand the command "husbands, love your wives" (Eph 5:25) as referring to the emotional relationship between husband and wife. In fact, Paul is here commanding husbands to serve and care for their wives, even as Jesus served and cared for the church by giving his life as a sacrifice.

## Emotion Words in the Bible

The second area of misunderstanding involves words in scripture—such as joy, mourning, anger, fear, zeal, compassion—which clearly do refer in some way to emotions. The misunderstanding arises because people living in biblical times did not understand these words in the same way that we do today.

The essential meaning of emotion-words in scripture (words that describe behavior which we would see as emotional behavior) could be described in the following way: these words refer primarily to emphatic objective responses to situations, often, but not necessarily, accompanied by corresponding subjective dispositions. The modern understanding of these words focuses almost exclusively on their subjective aspects, but the biblical psychology is more concerned with the objective behavior described by these words.

Emotion-words in scripture are tied closely to the external situations which evoke them. For example, rejoicing occurs in response to some blessing from God: "The most frequent occasions for joy are feasting and offering sacrifice (Dt 12:11-14; Is 56:7), celebrating harvest or victory (1 Sm 18:6; Jl 1:16), enjoying prosperity or personal triumph as seen especially in the recovery of health (Ps 31:7; Is 61:3-7); or rejoicing in God as part of public worship."[1] Similarly, mourning is a response to sin or disaster (Ez 9-10; Lam), anger and wrath a response to being wronged (Rom 2:5-11), and fear a response to being in the presence of a power far greater than oneself (Is 6; Jos 2:8-11). The emotion-words of scripture describe appropriate human *responses* to objective, external situations.

When people today use these words, they have something less objective in mind. The modern view of emotions sees them as potentially unrelated to external events. What we call joy and sorrow in modern society are sometimes responses to real circumstances, but just as often they are passing emotional states, a series of highs and lows that punctuate a person's life regardless of his or her circumstances. Emotions are seen as irrational and unpredictable subjective events, sometimes pleasant and sometimes bothersome. Rarely are they viewed as responses to external situations.

## *External Responses*

The emotion-words found in scripture refer not only to responses to objective situations; they refer to expressions which are objective, external, and intelligible within a given culture. Once again, rejoicing and mourning provide an especially vivid example:

> Physical expression of joy is often mentioned [in scripture]. Expressions which occur most frequently in connection with the terms for rejoicing are the sounds of singing, shouting, noise, uproar, a loud voice, singing praise; words for musical instruments . . . dancing, clapping, leaping, or stamping feet.[2]

> It was the Israelite practice to express festive joy by washing, anointing, and the wearing of a clean festal garment; the expression of grief was the abandonment of the tokens of joy and the adoption of their opposite: soiling the person, wearing of old garments, and loud, stylized cries of grief.[3]

Other concrete expressions of mourning involved rending garments (2 Sm 1:2), wearing sackcloth (2 Sm 3:31), covering the head (2 Sm 15:30), walking barefoot (2 Sm 15:30), gesturing wildly (Jer 31:19), and fasting (1 Sm 31:13).

The other emotion-words of scripture also have their characteristic behavioral expressions. Fear is expressed in hiding the face (Ex 3:6), keeping distance (Ex 20:18-21), prostrating oneself and bowing (Lk 24:5; Rv 1:17), obedience (Ex 20:20), and similar customs of respect (the word "respect" in English is often used to translate the Hebrew and Greek words for fear). The words for anger and wrath often could be translated as "punishment" without widely missing the mark; they refer as much to disciplinary *action* as they do to an internal state of rage: "In most New Testament passages *orge* (wrath) is in fact the divine work, destiny, or judgment of wrath. . . . As in the Old Testament, so the New Testament *orge* is both God's displeasure at evil, his passionate resistance to every will which is set against him, and also his judicial attack thereon."[4] The word for zeal refers to aggressive action in defense of a relationship or in defense of the honor of one's name, rather than to a feeling of enthusiasm or resolution (Jn 2:13-17).

The modern approach to these emotions is very different. They are mainly viewed as internal states that may or may not be expressed in culturally intelligible forms of behavior. The essence of joy, mourning, anger, fear, or zeal is a feeling that is passively experienced. I am rejoicing if I feel joyful, regardless of whether I sing, shout, and dance on a tabletop, or simply crouch in a corner and ponder the happy, tingling sensation happening somewhere inside me.

This brings us to the root of biblical psychology and the main difference in psychological makeup between biblical and modern people. The psychology of human beings in Western societies today is built on a set of distinctions possible only to a highly introspective, abstract, and analytical mentality—the distinctions between thought, emotion, will, and action. For the man or woman of the twentieth century, to think, feel, choose, and act is to exercise different faculties which perform distinct functions.

These distinctions are totally alien to the men and women of the Old and New Testaments. They viewed ideas, feelings, decisions, actions, and even the consequences of actions as connected steps in one continuous process of moral activity.

According to European psychology action first originates in the region of ideas; then it is penetrated by feeling, which in its turn makes it to be determined by volition; this again leads to resolution, which is followed by action. Thus the activity of the soul is completed; the result of the action lies entirely outside its sphere, being added as a new element. The one who acts trusts to his good intentions and feels no responsibility regarding the result, as long as the intentions were good.

For the Israelite . . . the mental processes are not successive, but united in one, because the soul is always a unit, acting in one. But no more are the action and its result to be distinguished from each other or from the mental activities; they are implied in the actual mental process. This is to be attributed to the fact that the soul is wholly present in all its works. The actions are not sent away from the soul, they are the outer manifestations of the whole of the soul, the traces of its movements; its 'ways' the Hebrew calls them.[5]

To the internal events of thinking, feeling, and willing there is tied not only the external action but also the result of the action, and therefore "the man is responsible for his acts and their results, not only for his intentions."[6] For the man or woman of biblical times, the subjective and objective worlds, the internal and the external spheres, were closely united. And it was the objective and external world that was the touchstone for judging the genuineness of the internal and the subjective.

For the people of the scripture, emotion-words referred to observable and intelligible behavior. Feelings of joy or fear that were not expressed in commonly understood cultural forms were not genuine joy or fear. The emotion-words of scripture do not describe subjective states isolatable from the realm of objective human behavior, passively experienced feelings separable from thought, will, action, and social intercourse. Instead, they describe visible human behavior involving the entire person.

## Appropriate vs. Authentic

The emotion-words of scripture thus refer primarily to objectively expressed responses to objective external situations. Often the response corresponds to an internal subjective state. The people of Israel tremble before Sinai's lightning, thunder, and smoke, and obviously experience a fear that penetrates to their bones' marrow. Moses did not need to decide to respond angrily when he first saw his people making merry before the golden calf: his rage was immediate, spontaneous, and impassioned.

However, there are other instances in scripture in which people are called to rejoice or to fear regardless of their internal state. A fine example of this is found in the eighth chapter of Nehemiah. A body of exiles have returned to Jerusalem, and they gather together in holy assembly to hear the reading of the law. The words of scripture—perhaps the stern commands and curses of the Pentateuch—cut them to the heart, and they begin to weep. The leaders of the assembly are taken aback by this response, and see it as inappropriate to the occasion: " 'This day is holy to the Lord your God; do not mourn or weep. . . . Go your way, eat the fat and drink sweet wine and send portions to him for whom nothing is prepared; for this day is holy to our Lord; and do not be grieved, for the joy of the Lord is your strength.' . . . And all the people went their way to eat and drink and to send portions and to make great rejoicing" (Neh 8:9, 10, 12).

The feeling most immediately stirred in the people is grief, and they express it with tears. Learning that this is an inappropriate response, they follow the direction of their leaders and begin to rejoice—to eat, drink, and celebrate. The leaders do not command the people to *feel* differently (though food, wine, and song will usually accomplish this purpose), but to express the objectively appropriate response to the occasion.

This approach runs directly counter to the modern ideal of authenticity. According to this ideal, one should never express something that one does not feel. It is dishonest and inauthentic to rejoice with your actions if you do not feel like rejoicing. One must be "true to one's self," with "one's self" meaning "one's feelings."

The Bible knows nothing of this ideal of authenticity. It instead presumes that one's expressed emotional responses should be governed by appropriateness to the situation rather than by personal inclination. Feeling is not only intimately connected to action, it is also intimately connected to will and judgment.

## 2000 Years of Change

Thus, the psychological outlook that has evolved in the modern world differs drastically from the outlook of scriptural times. Massive changes in culture have occurred in the two millenia or more since scripture was written, changes in personality as well as changes in values, customs, and social structure. Though the historical forces underlying this cultural evolution are enormously complex, a few strands in the process can be isolated.

First, there has been progressive historical movement away from a corporate, unself-conscious, and universalistic culture and toward an individualistic, introspective, and relativistic culture. The process of cultural change has tended toward (1) individualism—an erosion of communal and familial structures in favor of more atomistic structures; (2) introspection—a greater preoccupation with individual internal experience; and (3) relativism—a breakdown of absolute standards of morality and truth in favor of more fluid and flexible norms. This progression can be charted across most of the key Western cultural milieus inhabited by Christians over the past twenty centuries—through Jewish, Hellenistic, Medieval, Renaissance, Enlightenment, and Romantic cultures, all the way to twentieth-century Western culture.

With regard to the first aspect of change—the erosion of communal and familial structures—the more recent development of technological society has meant the loss of key communal structures in which emotions were traditionally expressed. As impersonal bureaucratic structures increasingly dominate public life, there is a weakening of the communal groupings, such as the nuclear family, the extended family, the neighborhood cluster, and the local church, which formerly provided a cultural context for the expression of mourning, rejoicing, affection, anger and punishment, and fear and respect. This breakdown of communal groupings leads to the loss of any commonly understood cultural language for expressing emotions.

In addition, the modern reaction against the impersonality of technological society also leads to a new focus on emotions. As has been pointed out, large organizations valuing skill and efficency rather than personal relationships have replaced the natural community. This depersonalization of public life has taken its toll on individuals, forcing them to place greater importance on their emotions, particularly in private life." People react strongly against role expectations in private life. Forced to behave in public life according to objective role requirements which take little account of how they feel, people rebel against behaving this way in private. This reaction to technological society lies at the root of the modern ideal of authenticity.

Finally, modern society has seen an apparent increase in serious psychological and emotional disorders. Our society is riddled by suicide, drug addiction, violent crime, and emotional problems such as depression and anxiety. These disorders are a sign of a psychological change in our society and also a factor adding to the great preoccupation with emotions. When psychological adjustment and emotional health become the conscious goals of most people in society, one can anticipate a heightened level of introspection.

## Significance

Several conclusions can be drawn from this presentation of biblical psychology and its approach to emotions.

First, we need a basic understanding of biblical psychology if we are to avoid many popular misinterpretations of biblical teaching. For example, scripture contains many commands that use *emotion-words*: "rejoice always," "fear the Lord," "delight in the law," "mourn for your sins." The modern tendency is to concentrate on cultivating proper emotional states of joy, fear, delight, and sorrow. This practice is not forbidden in the Bible, probably because it was inconceivable to the writers of scripture. Though not forbidden, this cultivation of emotional states is clearly not the intention of the biblical commands.

Second, biblical psychology is necessarily connected to biblical sociology, just as modern psychology is connected to modern sociology. The approach to emotions manifested in scripture fits the highly communal pattern of life shared by people of scriptural times. It fits a society that has clear social norms and moral standards. It presumes the existence of a commonly understood cultural language for expressing emotions. Therefore, any attempt to regain something of a biblical psychology should be joined to an attempt to regain something of a biblical sociology. And one could also argue conversely that any attempt to restore something of a scriptural communal life should also pay attention to the scriptural approach to emotions which supports that communal life.

Third, Christian leaders today should at least consider the possibility of restoring some aspects of biblical psychology. The circumstances of technological society appear to create profound psychological and emotional disorders in large numbers of people, and modern introspective therapies have a less than glorious record of success in treating these disorders. The biblical approach to psychology and emotions, that is, the approach which scripture presumes, could offer some helpful insights. Certainly we could never reshape ourselves psychologically into eighth-century B.C. Judaean merchants, nor should we attempt to do so. Still, there may be important aspects of the biblical psychology that would prove immensely helpful in our modern circumstances.

To put the massive cultural changes of the past 2000 years in proper perspective, one should recognize that modern psychology is a far greater historical novelty than biblical psychology. Earlier we imagined ourselves entertaining an ancient Israelite and marveling at the unique features of his temperament. Perhaps we should also imagine his response to our strange habits and introspective quirks of personality. He would marvel as greatly as we. The oddity all depends on one's point of view.

# TWO

# A Pastoral Strategy

WHEN PASTORAL LEADERS look at their congregations and Christian groups to see what's happening in the area of emotions, what do they encounter? The most noticeable thing, particularly in our country but to some extent throughout the Western world, is that the focus is increasingly on emotional life. People devote a lot of effort to figuring out what their desires and fears are, whether others like them, whether they have the confidence to handle a situation, or why they feel guilty or angry. In general, people are very concerned about their emotions.

This focus on feelings is widespread among Christian leaders as well as among those they are guiding. For instance, some Christian programs for marriage enrichment place a heavy emphasis on married couples communicating their feelings. In order to share about their feelings intensively, couples have to spend time thinking about their feelings and selecting the right images to describe them. Some programs feature various techniques to help couples do this.

Some Christian leaders place a great emphasis on feelings not only in marriage but in other relationships as well. Sharing about feelings becomes the mark of authenticity. "Reporting your 'gut-level feelings,' " one Christian author writes, is "the basic communication of a deep loving relationship."

Christians have picked up this attitude from the society around them, where concentration on feelings has been developing in the last couple of decades or so. Today secular psychologists are saying things like the following: "Being in touch with your feelings is the only way you can ever become your highest self, the only way you can become open and free, the only way you can become your own person. . . . If you don't live in your feelings, you don't live in the real world. Feelings are the truth."[7] This example may seem fairly extreme, but it represents a trend in contemporary society.

One reason for the trend has to do with the technological nature of contemporary society, which has deeply affected how people relate to one another. Human beings were made to be in social relationships within communities, and formerly most people lived and worked in some kind of natural community. This more personal world has been transformed by the coming of modern technology and business; natural community has been replaced with large organizations and bureaucracies which value skill and efficiency rather than personal relationships. In reaction to this depersonalization of public life, people have come to place a heightened importance on their emotions, especially in private life.

It can help to realize that the situation we face today is not typical of every group of people at every period of history. Rather, this focus on feelings is a feature of contemporary technological society.

Because the Christians we are caring for are immersed in a society which puts undue concentration on feelings, we must pay more attention to helping people handle their feelings than the pastors and teachers of the New Testament communities had to do. The New Testament itself makes only occasional references to emotional life. It talks about the emotions here and there, but nowhere in the New Testament—or in all the Bible— are the emotions dealt with extensively. This reflects the pastoral situation. People in the cultures in which the scriptures were written did not believe that feelings are the truth or that all meaning in life depends on the emotions or that understanding and sharing about feelings is the best way to form deep bonds between human beings. Even though the New Testament does not have a great concern with the emotions in and of themselves, our cultural situation impels us to pay special attention to the subject.

## *Repression*

Let us look more closely at how the people in our care think about their emotions. People latch on to a variety of current views of emotional life. I am going to lump these views into two categories.

If you try to analyze how members of your congregation or group handle their emotions, you will probably find that some of them think negatively of their emotions and regard their feelings as dangerous. When they experience an emotion, such as anger or seductive desire, they may respond automatically by repressing it, pushing it down inside without much thought. Or they may try to get rid of the feeling by sheer willpower.

This negative approach to the emotions differs from the preoccupation with feelings I have been describing. It is not the prevailing trend in today's society. But it is worth mentioning because many people, especially Christians, still treat their feelings this way, at least some of the time.

For example, I know many Christians who think that anger is always wrong. Some of them even believe that scripture teaches this. Of course, as the passage I quoted from Paul makes clear, scripture teaches that anger can sometimes be an acceptable reaction, and that it is how we respond to the reaction that is either good or bad.

## *Emotionalism*

The second approach that people take is to stand in awe of their emotions. For example, some people believe that life is an emotional flow; the way to handle it is to float along like driftwood. Wherever their emotions carry them is where they go to find meaning. Others have become fine-tuned to their feelings, exquisitely introspective, always sorting out what is happening in their emotions. Still others have been taught to indulge their emotions, or by the absence of proper training have never learned not to indulge them.

Various pop-psychological movements encourage the unrestrained expression of feelings. For example, I know someone who was very fearful of anger and dealt with it by repressing it. Then she joined a TA group which told her that anger is good and that she ought to express it unrestrainedly. She began to express her anger by going into her basement for hours at a time and kicking around two pillows, one labeled "John," the other, "Mike"—the leaders of a prayer group she belonged to. Eventually her unrestrained emotionalism disrupted all her Christian relationships and she broke off membership in her church.

Some people combine a repressive approach in an area such as anger with an emotion-dominated approach in other areas, for example, impulsiveness in how they spend their time and money.

## The Biblical Way

Neither repressing emotions out of fear nor allowing them to dominate constitutes the scriptural way. We need to give people sound teaching that will provide them with a scriptural understanding of what the emotions are and how God intends them to function.

I would express a basic scriptural principle regarding the emotions this way: *God intends to transform people so that their emotions instinctively support them in righteous living.* Let us look at some of the implications of this statement.

First of all, emotions are to be *supportive.* In Jesus' life and the lives of men and women in scripture who are held up for our imitation, we see the emotions functioning in ways that help them to do God's will. Sometimes particular emotions actually enable someone to do what is right. For example, anger aroused Paul to rightly exercise spiritual authority in a situation where it was dangerous for him to do so (see Acts 16:16-18, the exorcising of the fortune-telling spirit); anger moved him to preach the gospel where he had not intended to (see Acts 17:16-33, Paul preaches in Athens). Grief spurred Ezra and those who had returned from exile to take measures against a problem of intermarriage (see Ezr 9-10).

Elsewhere in scripture, particular emotions are merely part of a right human response to various situations. When Jesus came to Lazarus' tomb he wept, even though he already knew that Lazarus had died and that he himself would raise him. Sorrow was simply the appropriate human response to the death of his friend. Similarly, Jesus felt compassion when he met people who were sick or possessed, anger when he encountered opposition to God's kingdom, joy when he saw God's kingdom preached with power.

God has created the full range of emotional reactions that people have, and each emotion has a purpose. Even those which seem to be destructive or negative, like anger and fear, are intended to be helpful. Anger can help people deal successfully with difficulties or opposition. Fear can help them by warning of danger.

When scripture counsels us regarding our emotions it is referring to actions and behavior, not primarily to feelings. For example, when it tells us not to be afraid, it is instructing us not to give in to fear; it is not condemning the emotional reaction itself. In the same way, Jesus' teaching that a man not look lustfully at a woman instructs us that we should not misdirect our sexual desires, but Jesus does not condemn sexual desire itself.

This touches on an important distinction: there is a difference between the emotional reaction a person experiences and the way the person responds to that reaction. Scripture never makes this distinction explicit; rather, as in the passage about looking lustfully, it assumes the distinction.

In practice it is sometimes difficult to distinguish where the emotional reaction ends and the response begins. But it is important to show people that in principle there is a difference.

The scriptural approach to the emotions assumes that, while we may experience various emotional reactions, we should learn to handle our emotional responses righteously. As we allow God's word to shape our responses, we can expect him to change our emotional reactions so that they become more supportive of our efforts to do his will.

The second implication of the basic principle is that emotions are to support the Christian in *righteous* living. Scripture clearly teaches that people's emotional reactions must be subordinated to God's intentions—to his standards of righteousness, to his intentions for a particular situation, to the rule of love.

In the gospels we see that Jesus handled his anger differently according to what was right for different situations. On one occasion in a synagogue he became angry at the Pharisees when they would not answer his challenge as to whether it was right to save life on the sabbath. "He looked around at them with anger, grieved at their hardness of heart, and said to the man, 'Stretch out your hand.'" He did not let his anger distract him from what God wanted him to do—to heal the man's hand (Mk 3:1-6). On another occasion he plaited ropes into a whip and drove the money changers from the temple. He knew that it was appropriate for him to express his anger that way. In both cases the Lord subordinated his anger to what God wanted to accomplish. He was in control of his anger; his anger was not in control of him.

Similarly, after Pentecost Jesus' disciples subordinated fear to what God wanted them to do. Fear did not determine their decisions. If a situation called for action, they acted with boldness and courage, even when there was an element of risk. For example, the apostles who spoke freely about the Lord Jesus were in danger in Jerusalem, and they probably knew fear. But they also knew that they needed to do what God called them to do.

The third implication is that emotions are to *instinctively* support people in righteous living. God wants to change people so that their emotions generally operate instinctively to support

Christian living. In other words, once their emotions are working right, people should not have to stop and reflect on their feelings before they act. Jesus did not have to stop and think about getting angry, about how to use his anger, about whether it was right to use it. He got angry and used his anger instinctively to do the right thing.

The last implication concerns *transformation*. If people are going to experience their emotions as supports in living the Christian life, their emotions are going to have to change. Primarily this means that people will have to grow in Christian character, which involves, among other things, experiencing personal transformation in the ways they respond emotionally. As a result of this maturity, their instinctive reactions to stimuli will usually be helpful.

The assurance that this kind of change is possible flies in the face of the contemporary conviction that "feelings are the truth" and that emotions are the facts of life that shape behavior. This deterministic view is implicit in many psychological therapies which assume that people are programmed to act in certain ways by their past, particularly by their parents. Usually these therapies see the emotions as the vehicle through which the determinism of the past expresses itself—in anger, fear, low self-esteem, and so on. Scripture, however, leads us to expect that a person's responses to emotional reactions can change.

Consider the example of Peter. Out of fear on the eve of the Lord's crucifixion, Peter fled and denied the Lord three times. Yet after the resurrection, a change occurred in Peter, and by the power of the Holy Spirit he was able to speak publicly about the Lord, to work miracles in Jerusalem, and to face squarely the threats that were made against him. I am not saying that Peter never experienced fear again, but simply that by the power of the Spirit he was changed so that he was able to deal with fear courageously. Christians can deal with fear courageously and can learn to respond in the right way to all their emotional reactions.

## *Perspective*

As this character change takes place, a corresponding change in emotional reactions often occurs. The reaction of fear, for example, lessens or disappears in certain situations. My experience in various Christian groups suggests, however, that change on this level does not reach completion in every area of a person's life. Christians can expect that they will have to live with some degree of difficulty in certain of their emotional reactions. The emotional aspects of the conflict between the flesh and the Spirit will not come entirely to an end, and it is helpful to communicate realistic expectations in this regard.

It also helps to communicate a scriptural perspective on this fact. We should help people to adopt the scriptural view that Christians ought to be concerned primarily with growing in Christian character—bearing the fruit of the Spirit—not with smoothing out all their emotional reactions.

## *Strategy for Change*

We need a strategy for helping people experience change in their emotional life. I believe the essence of the strategy can be stated very simply: *If people are "in Christ" a power is at work in their lives to change them for the better.* The key to order in the emotions is to be united to Christ.

Paul writes, "Now the Lord is the Spirit, and where the Spirit of the Lord is, there is freedom. And we all, with unveiled face, beholding the glory of the Lord, are being changed into his likeness from one degree of glory to another; for this comes from the Lord who is the Spirit" (2 Cor 3:17-18). When people are in a personal relationship with Christ, they are united with the Holy Spirit. He takes them as they are, changes them, and produces in them more and more of the character of Jesus Christ. The change goes on simply because of union with Christ and the Holy Spirit. It is something that happens by the power of the Spirit, almost without anyone paying attention to it.

Therefore pastoral leaders can expect that people's emotional lives will change simply because the Holy Spirit is in those who are in Christ.

To be in Christ also means to be in a whole new social environment, a new set of personal relationships with brothers and sisters, called the body of Christ. Within the context of these new relationships, as men and women who love one another, people's emotional lives will become better and more wholesome all the time.

This strategy for helping people with their emotions has four main characteristics. Let's look at them.

*First, this approach fixes attention not on people's own efforts but on God's work within people to change their emotional life.*

Suppose we teach the Christians in our care about the scriptural view of the emotions. They may already realize that their emotions need to change, and now they hear that they *can* change. The first thing that many of them will do is to set up an agenda for self-improvement; they will try their hardest to get the change to happen on their own. But this do-it-yourself approach can undermine the process of change.

If a person who has a problem with repression tries to get his or her emotional life in order by sheer willpower, that person will probably not experience any degree of success. If someone who gives too much attention and sway to their emotions tries to get their emotional life in order by giving it a lot of attention, they will probably wind up being even more introspective.

God's way of dealing with people's emotional life is to change it by the power of the Spirit. Of course, they are going to have to make some decisions along the way—deciding to love, repenting of wrongdoing, putting relationships right, and so on. These are ways of cooperating with God. But change happens primarily as God initiates it by the power of his Spirit and through personal relationships in the local expression of the body of Christ.

So it is important when teaching about the emotions to guide people away from a self-help program and to help them place their attention on God's work; their faith should be in his action rather than in their efforts to change.

*Second, this approach involves teaching people that their conduct should be determined by whatever is the right and loving thing to do, not by their emotional reactions.*

As I have pointed out, the contemporary trend is for people to be concerned with understanding how they feel, with expressing their feelings, with understanding how others feel. All this leads people subtly or shamelessly into being dominated by their feelings. Instead, we should teach people to adopt the scriptural perspective, in which people's behavior—whether it is loving or unloving, right or wrong—is the most important factor.

How many times have we heard that living according to one's feelings is liberating and that living according to an objective standard is repressive? But that view is false and its antithesis is true. Living according to one's feelings imprisons a person; it makes feelings the master. Scripture gives no reason to believe that emotions are particularly well-suited for governing people's lives. Emotional reactions are irrational and unstable; they are a part of human nature which can sometimes come into conflict with God's will and which, therefore, must not be in control. To be dominated by one's feelings is the opposite of freedom. The objective standards of behavior that scripture provides are a means to freedom. They show the way to freedom as a person moves from the vagaries of feelings into behavior which is based on God's intentions for human life.

The first step to emotional health is taken when someone decides that no matter how they feel, they are going to do what is right, what God wants them to do. That person should regard his or her emotions as helpful when they support that decision and unreliable when they don't. To teach people this is to teach them the Christian doctrine of repentance. It is to instruct them in what Paul calls "walking by the Spirit" (Gal 5:16, 25), "walking as children of light" (Eph 5:8), "putting off the old nature and putting on the new nature" (Col 3:9-10), "putting to death what is earthly in us" (Col 3:5). Whether God's standards of behavior are freeing rather than repressive depends upon a person's decision to obey them from the heart. If someone tries to live according to God's revealed standards out of fear of disapproval or some kind of compulsion, God's standards will seem oppressive, and the person will have to repress various feelings. However, if a person chooses from the heart to follow the Lord's standards, those standards can be the route to emotional freedom.

So we should help people to make a decision from the heart to follow the truth. In doing so, we will often have to clear up a misunderstanding. Nowadays when people use the word "heart" they mean their feelings. But the biblical use of the term is different. In scripture, the heart is the seat of fundamental decision and orientation in a person's life. It is deeper than the emotions, the intellect, and the will. It is the very core of the person. What a person decides in his or her heart orients everything else that he or she wills to do. The will implements the decisions of the heart.

When a person decides from the heart to follow the Lord's commands, he or she can overcome substantial emotional difficulties. Several years ago I met a young man who had gotten so deeply mired in his feelings that he was hospitalized for part of his senior year in high school with psychosomatic illnesses. He was following his desires into various kinds of immorality and living an entirely subjective life. Shortly after he became a Christian, he received instruction that encouraged him to set his heart on loving God and loving his brothers and sisters in Christ. He decided to follow the instruction. I have never seen anyone do it with such ruthlessness. Within two years he became free of the major emotional problems that afflicted his earlier teenage life.

*Third, this strategy, which is based on God's work in the believer, involves teaching people to deal with their emotions with faith in their authority as sons and daughters of God.*

We should teach people to have faith in the change that has come about through their adoption as God's sons and daughters. If the Christian has been given a new nature as scripture says, if he lives in the Spirit, if he has crucified the flesh, then he can live a new life.

Many Christians think that they lack the power or the resources to live a new life in Christ. When they encounter an emotional difficulty, they conclude that they need special help. While Christians ought to turn to the Lord for help and do sometimes need special counsel and support, it is a mistake for them to approach emotional problems with a conviction of inadequacy. The power to deal with the problem, the power that can make the change, is already in them. The Lord has given them the authority to deal with emotional difficulties and to make the changes that are necessary.

A Christian ought to approach emotional problems in much the same way that a teacher would handle an unruly classroom. The teacher would not proceed by constantly laying down the law; that would provoke the children to greater rebellion. She would lay down the law about those things that were intolerable; for the rest she would gradually and firmly bring order into the situation.

For example, take someone who is having difficulty controlling his anger. It may be that the person is trying to meet too many commitments. Unable to handle the demands upon him, he becomes frustrated and angry. Instead of exerting his will to repress his anger, to "lay down the law" to himself, he should act decisively to sort out his commitments and to cut back on certain activities. Such a step will bring order into an otherwise disordered life and will strike effectively at the real source of anger.

Christians can also exercise authority over their emotions with a word of rebuke. Faced with unruly feelings—fear, for example—a Christian can tell himself that he is a son of God, living in obedience to God by the power God supplies, and that unruly feelings will have to submit to that authority.

Exercising this kind of authority can be compared to a citizen asserting his legal rights. For example, in a confrontation with someone trying to injure or defraud him, a citizen does not have to rely on his own physical ability, which might be insufficient to overpower his opponent. Instead he can be confident of obtaining justice because he knows he has the authority of the law behind him.

This exercise of authority is not the same as the willpower approach, which is hostile to the emotions and fears them. The Christian recognizes that the emotions are basically good; he simply refuses to be intimidated by them when they seem very strong and urge him to turn from God's will. He asserts that, because he is a son of God in whom the Holy Spirit is at work, he is going to be able to do the right thing, and he is confident that, because he is under God's authority, his emotions are going to come into line.

*Fourth, the strategy means that we must teach Christians to relate to one another as members of the body of Christ.*

As I have said, living in a community of Christians who love one another is an important aspect of what scripture means by being "in Christ," and it is a key to experiencing the power of Christ in our lives. Change in a person's emotional life comes in part from being in the body of Christ, being in a community of loving relationships.

Because that is true, Christians need to be taught to relate well to one another and to support emotional healing and growth in their brothers and sisters. For example, we should teach people that they should repent when they fall into bad behavior as a consequence of mishandling their emotional reactions. Someone who is touchy or full of self-pity or withdrawn or depressed is very likely affecting people in his or her environment and ought to repent of that behavior.

Many other examples of behavior that affects emotional health could be cited. Christians should not manipulate one another by playing on guilt feelings. They should learn how to control anger so that it does not damage relationships. They need to be taught to be encouraging in their speech and to express affection to one another. They should learn how to admonish someone who does something wrong, rather than holding it in and becoming resentful. They need to learn how to live in faith, hope, and love rather than immersing themselves in criticalness and complaining.

## Tips for Teaching

Let me conclude this chapter with some suggestions about how to design teaching for Christians that will communicate the kind of biblical perspective on the emotions which I have been discussing.

First, it helps to explain the scriptural approach by contrasting it with other ways people think about and deal with their feelings. For instance:

—*repression.* Repression is different from control. It is based on the person's fear that he or she cannot handle something. It involves burying something and keeping it out of sight, rather than finding the right place for it.

—*willpower alone.* The exercise of the will is not out of place in the scriptural approach, but "willpower alone" is wrong because of what it leaves out—God's power and our faith in it. It ignores the necessity for us not only to turn our will to God's ways but to turn our heart to him also.

—*emotional determinism.* Scripture does not authenticate the approach that "my feelings are the way I am." The biblical view involves belief that change is possible.

—*stoicism.* Stoicism says, in effect, that emotional reactions are obstacles to right living, and that the more people get free of emotional reactions the better they are. But Christians understand that God gave us the ability to react emotionally.

—*introspectiveness.* It is true that it can sometimes help to glance inward. But a habit of introspectiveness does not bring self-knowledge. Self-knowledge comes from objective as well as subjective sources, such as observing our behavior, listening to what others tell us about ourselves, understanding spiritual realities like the conflict of the flesh and the Spirit within us. Self-knowledge is generally helpful in overcoming emotional difficulties, introspection more rarely so. In fact, while introspection can occasionally be useful, introspectiveness is an emotional problem.

Second, it helps to point out that some approaches to emotions treat feelings as *enemies* (repression, willpower alone, stoicism) while others treat them as *masters* (emotional determinism, introspection, impulsiveness). But the Christian view is that the emotions should be *servants* in our lives, supporting us in living as God wants us to. This terminology lends itself to analogies and images that can help to clarify the teaching. The life of Jesus particularly, and the lives of other biblical figures such as Paul, offer many illustrations of the emotions functioning as servants—generally helpful, always subordinate.

Third, various analogies and parables can also help explain Christians' authority over their emotional life. I have already mentioned the analogy of the teacher who gradually but firmly brings order into her classroom. The difference between exercising authority and using willpower alone can be explained by means of a legal analogy. For example, a landlord who has some destructive and abusive tenants might go to them and tell them that they have to improve their behavior. He could do this confidently even if they outnumber him and are stronger than he, because he owns the apartment building and knows that the authority of the law stands behind his insistence that they live up to the rental agreement.

Such an analogy could explain how a person would deal with feelings of fear which make it difficult for him to relate to people in various situations. The person might remind himself that although he feels fearful and awkward in certain social settings, God has given him authority to go ahead and do whatever is right, that is, to act confidently. He could confront his fear with the assurance that he has the power of the Holy Spirit.

A final comment concerning teaching Christians about the emotions: to do so will generally make the pastoral leader more sensitive to issues in the congregation or Christian group regarding how people relate to one another, the quality of committed love among them, and the degree to which they understand Christian teaching about behavior and relationships. These are issues to take seriously.

In the first two chapters we have considered a biblical perspective and presented a pastoral strategy for the emotions. The following chapters provide advice for helping people control and use specific emotions in their Christian life.

## We Can Be Changed

Most Christians need to battle regularly with unruly desires. It is therefore crucial that pastoral leaders know how to help people overcome their desires and live in righteousness, love, and the Holy Spirit. It is also useful for pastoral leaders to know how to help people grow in the Lord so that their unruly desires change into or become overshadowed by submissive, supportive spiritual desires.

Christians need not resign themselves fatalistically to a state of perpetual conflict with rebellious and unrighteous desires. As people mature in Christ their "constellation of desires" should gradually change so that they more and more coincide with God's desires. We may never reach perfect harmony between our desires and God's but substantial change is possible.

Unfortunately, some Christians try to change their desires in a way that does as much damage as good. This happens when people recognize that they have a strong desire for something that others would find shameful or repulsive. They then decide to change this desire in order to avoid social disapproval. A serious internal conflict then arises. The reason for the conflict is that they have not actually renounced the old desire from the heart; their predominant concern is merely to escape ostracism. They are reacting to an external pressure rather than choosing a deep-seated internal change.

I have seen this pattern of conflict develop among people having problems with sexual desires—a habit of reading pornographic magazines, for instance. The person who wants to change merely to avoid social stigma experiences little progress and intense internal conflict. On the other hand, the person who wants to change because of a desire to please God might put the habit aside fairly simply. The key lies in a genuine change of heart.

You will remember that scripture views the heart as the core of the human person, the seat of one's fundamental orientation in life. The heart has thoughts (Heb 4:12), intentions (Heb 4:12), and purposes (1 Cor 4:5).

Jesus speaks of the heart in Matthew 12:33-35:

> Either make the tree good, and its fruit good; or make the tree bad, and its fruit bad; for the tree is known by its fruit. You brood of vipers! How can you speak good, when you are evil? For out of the heart the mouth speaks. The good man out of his good treasure brings forth good, and the evil man out of his evil treasure brings forth evil.

The heart is the source from which all speech and action sprout, like fruit growing from a tree. And significant and lasting change must begin with the heart.

A person who renounces a particular desire from the heart can experience a gradual reorientation of his or her set of desires. This is not a repression of desires in reaction to an externally imposed pressure, but a fundamental reordering of desire that begins at the center of one's life and flows outwards.

# THREE

# Desiring What God Desires

R ANDY WAS RAISED in a family of physicians, practicing or potential. Both his parents were doctors, and ever since childhood Randy and his brother wanted to become doctors also. When Randy went to college, he was certain he was heading toward a career in medicine.

As an undergraduate Randy became associated with a church in which the pastor took a special interest in him. Through the pastor's friendship, Randy's understanding of the gospel and Christian mission broadened and deepened. He involved himself heavily in various kinds of Christian service.

The pastor became convinced that Randy had exceptional gifts for evangelistic and pastoral ministry. It was clear that Randy could enter medical school and go on to become a fine doctor. But, the pastor urged him, he could do even more with his life if he prepared himself for a life of pastoral ministry.

Randy had never faced such an agonizing choice. He liked the evangelistic and pastoral work he had begun to do, but his desire to be a doctor, a desire that had developed throughout his life, was almost overwhelming. After several months of painful consideration, Randy finally decided to put medicine aside in order to train for full-time pastoral work.

## Desire: Two Views

Desire is a universal feature of human existence. Each of us has strong desires that color our thoughts and influence our decisions—desires for food, drink, sex, warmth, companionship, success, honor. Desire is the impulse to possess or enjoy something or someone, to accomplish a particular task or goal, to have a particular experience. It is also the inclination to avoid certain people, objects, tasks, and experiences.

Many Christians fall into extremes when they consider what part desires should play in their lives. On one side are the stoics, on the other side are the selfists.

Stoic Christians adopt the view, common in Greco-Roman philosophy, that desires are evil and should be uprooted. Their ideal of virtue is total detachment from material reality and human experience—including personal relationships, material possessions, and social status. Such Christians seek commitment only to God and to an abstract standard of conduct. This view is not so common among Christians today, but at one time it enjoyed a wide following.

More common among Christians now is the selfist attitude. According to this view, one's primary aim in life is to be self-fulfilled and well-adjusted, and the way to attain fulfillment is through the maximal satisfaction of one's desires. It is considered unhealthy to disregard or subordinate one's desires. At best, it is thought, such action will cause the true personality to wither away rather than blossom into full maturity. At worst, it is feared, repression of desires will produce serious psychological disorders. In the selfist view, satisfying our desires is crucial for our own health and growth and is also an act of love toward others because self-fulfillment and positive adjustment increase our contribution to society.

There are thus two extreme positions concerning desires. One is suspicious of and hostile to them, the other is sympathetic and favorable. Is either of these positions the Christian one? Let us look at the biblical teaching for guidance.

## Lusts

There are several words in the New Testament that convey the meaning of desire, longing, yearning. A study of one of the most frequently used of these words, *epithumia,* reveals the biblical teaching on desire.

*Epithumia* literally means to set one's heart or soul on something. It refers to an exceptionally strong desire. The word occurs over fifty times in various forms in the New Testament writings, with diverse connotations.

In many places *epithumia* carries a distinctively pejorative connotation. In these contexts the word refers to works of the flesh such as jealousy, enmity, covetousness, and desire for illicit sexual pleasures. It is sometimes translated "lust" or "passion": "Therefore God gave them up in the *lusts* of their hearts to impurity, to the dishonoring of their bodies" (Rom 1:24), and "each person is tempted when he is lured and enticed by his own *desire.* Then *desire* when it has conceived gives birth to sin; and sin when it is full grown brings forth death" (Jas 1:14-15). (For other examples, see Ti 3:3 and 1 Pt 1:14.)

Desires can obviously be very dangerous. The image in the first chapter of James is particularly graphic: *epithumia* is the mother of sin, which in turn is the mother of death.

A similar passage in 2 Peter speaks of our escaping from the "corruption that is in the world because of *passion*" (1:4), indicating the close relation between *epithumia* and death (a grandmother-grandaughter relationship, according to James). The stoic attitude to desires seems to be confirmed by these passages, sprinkled liberally throughout the New Testament.

## Godly Desires

However, there is another side to this word in the New Testament. *Epithumia* sometimes describes a godly and commendable desire, experienced by angels, prophets, apostles, and the Messiah himself. For instance:

"Truly, I say to you, many prophets and righteous men *longed* to see what you see, and did not see it" (Mt 13:17).

The things which have now been announced to you . . .

through the Holy Spirit sent from heaven, things into which angels *long* to look" (1 Pt 1:12).

"My *desire* is to depart and be with Christ" (Phil 1:23).

"And he said to them, 'I have *earnestly desired* to eat this passover with you before I suffer'" (Lk 22:15).

*Epithumia* is used in a particularly striking way in 1 Timothy 3:1, where Paul discusses the office of bishop: "If any one aspires to the office of bishop, he *desires* a noble task."

From these passages it is evident that *epithumia* is not always evil. In fact, it is portrayed as the right and proper response to that which is good, noble, and intrinsically desirable: the revelation of Christ, our heavenly life in God after death, the office of shepherd in God's church.

The stoic approach is unsound. The Lord does not want to liberate his people from all desires. Instead, he wants to free them from evil desires and to fill them with holy ones. The Lord disapproves of the "desires of the flesh," the passions of "our former ignorance," the sinful desires which characterize human nature apart from the redeeming grace of Jesus Christ. He does not disapprove of all human desires.

This distinction between two types of desires is further pointed up by the fact that when used negatively *epithumia* is often modified by terms which define the type of desires being condemned: ungodly (Jude 16-18), defiling (2 Pt 2:9-10), worldly (Ti 2:12), youthful (2 Tm 2:22), senseless and hurtful (1 Tm 6:9), licentious (2 Pt 2:18), deceitful (Eph 4:22), evil (Col 3:5), and fleshly (Rom 13:14; Gal 5:16-18, 24; Eph 2:3; 1 Pt 2:11, 18). Scripture does not condemn all desire, but instead rejects a particular type of desire, the type that governs human nature when it is alienated from the life of God.

## Disordered Desires

From the biblical point of view, there are two main problems with human desires. The first problem concerns the object of desire. As a consequence of the fall, human desires have become twisted and distorted so that we commonly desire things which are both harmful for us and displeasing to God.

This is what Paul means when he says that "the desires of the flesh are against the Spirit, and the desires of the Spirit are against the flesh" (Gal 5:17). The desires of sinful human nature lead to what Paul calls the "works of the flesh": "fornication, impurity, licentiousness, idolatry, sorcery, enmity, strife, jealousy, anger, selfishness, dissension, party spirit, envy, drunkenness, carousing, and the like" (Gal 5:19-21).

The desires imparted by the Holy Spirit directly oppose the desires of the rebellious flesh. The Spirit imparts a desire for righteousness, prayer, love of the brethren, knowledge of God, and the second coming of Christ. Desire is not the problem: it is the object of desire that is the problem.

However, in another sense, desire itself is the problem. The fall of the human race led not only to a distortion in the objects of our desires, but also to a disorder in the nature of desire itself. Desire became unruly, ungovernable, determined to rule and direct and control. Formerly valuable as a servant, desire now became man's lord.

We ourselves were once foolish, disobedient, led astray, slaves to various *passions* and pleasures. (Ti 3:3)

Whatever overcomes a man, to that he is enslaved. (2 Pt 2:19)

We once lived in the *passions* of our flesh, following the desires of body and mind, and so we were by nature children of wrath, like the rest of mankind. (Eph 2:3)

Other New Testament passages speak disparagingly of "following" our desires (Jude 16-18 and 2 Pt 3:3). Of course, this applies especially to the desires of the flesh. However, it is also true for more commendable spiritual desires. It is wrong for desires—even righteous ones—to rule and govern us.

This is evident from several verses in Paul's letter to the Philippians: "Yet which I shall choose I cannot tell. I am hard pressed between the two. My *desire* is to depart and be with Chrinced of this, I know that I shall remain and continue with you that is far better. Buall, for your progress and joy in the faith" the flesh is more necessary on your account. Conv(Phil 1:22-25).

Paul desires to depart from this life and be with the Lord. But he decides that it is better for him to remain in order to build up the church. Even such a holy and spiritual desire as this must be subjected to a higher standard of conduct—the standard of God's law of love. Thus, scripture teaches that desires should not automatically govern behavior, even when they are apparently virtuous and holy.

The biblical view of desires is neither stoic nor selfist. It neither condemns desires without qualification nor embraces them as the key to self-fulfillment and the infallible guide for human conduct. Desires can be helpful or harmful, holy or unholy, spiritual or fleshly. Even at its best, desire should not be the main factor determining human behavior.

## A Constructive Role

Desires can play a positive and constructive role in Christians' lives. When ordered properly, desires are gifts from God that motivate us to do what God wants us to do. It is good to have desires for prayer, scripture study, service, and evangelism. These desires support us in living as we ought to live.

Even basic biological desires are gifts from God. Our instinctive desire for food motivates us to find and ingest the nourishment that our bodies need to survive. Our desire for sex motivates us (ideally) to form and raise families which people the earth and transmit human life and culture from one generation to the next. These rudimentary biological desires can easily go wrong and lead people astray, but they need not do so. It is possible for all these desires to aid Christians in living for the Lord.

I know some Christians who think they have found a foolproof method for discerning the will of God for their lives:

whatever they desire most must *not* be God's will, and whatever they desire least must *certainly* be his will. Now, it must be acknowledged that the Lord often calls his servants to do things that run contrary to their preferences and desires, sometimes because their desires are disordered or misleading, sometimes because he wants to test their love and obedience. However, the conviction that God's will must always conflict with human desires is an inadequate rule of thumb for receiving divine guidance. When a Christian's life is in good order by the grace of God, his desires will often coincide with God's desires.

## Problems

Desires can also be a major hindrance to living for the Lord. They can make it very difficult for people to follow the commandments and the guidance of God. This most obviously applies to desires that have a sinful object: desires for sexual immorality, desires for drug-induced euphoria, desires to see others suffer. However, the Christian life can also be derailed by more neutral desires.

For example, Phil Boyer has a strong desire to work as a salesman for a particular pharmaceutical corporation. This desire is neutral in itself—intrinsically neither good or evil. If this desire leads Phil to accept a position involving the kind of traveling and overtime that would prevent him from caring properly for his wife and children or participating in the life of the church, then this neutral desire has probably ensnared Phil in a wrong decision.

Or again, Sarah Connors experiences a consuming desire to read mystery novels. The desire is neutral in itself (some may argue this point!). But if this desire leads Sarah to read novels each evening till two A.M. so that she is sleepy, distracted, and unfaithful in her responsibilities during the day, then this neutral desire has led Sarah off the track.

At times even virtuous and holy desires can hinder us from doing the will of God. I know a Christian man who has a remarkable love for prayer. Given the opportunity, he can pray for hours at a stretch without tremendous effort. This is unquestionably a wonderful God-given desire and ability. But it can get him into trouble. Once, when he worked as an administrator in a Christian organization, he was taking lengthy breaks and going to a local church to pray. As a result, he was accomplishing little at work. When admonished by his supervisor for his poor performance on the job, my friend suddenly realized that his fervent desire for prayer could actually pose a temptation needing to be resisted. Even the purest and most lofty desires can prevent Christians from accomplishing the will of God.

## Spiritual Disguises

One of the most subtle yet common ways that desires hinder Christians is by disguising themselves in spiritual or reasonable garb. When we allow this to mislead us, we are rationalizing. It is remarkable how ingenious we can be at devising spiritual and sober reasons to explain why we should do the things that we strongly desire to do.

I have often heard teenage couples say, "We really believe that God wants us together. We have prayed together, and have received assurance that this is his will." While God might conceivably give such guidance, common experience indicates that it is claimed more often than received. The source of the inspiration is more often Cupid than the Holy Spirit, yet it may be very difficult to persuade the young man and woman of this fact. "Oh, no, we are not together because of romantic or sexual desire! We are simply responding to the leading of the Lord." And, of course, they sincerely believe this.

This is the grave danger of rationalization—it involves not only deception of others but deception of ourselves. Human desires are shrewd and deceitful. They win their way as much through persuasion as through force. Strong desire disposes one to succumb even to shallow persuasion. Desire conquers, yet we may never fully realize that it has won—and that we have lost.

If Christians are to maximize the good and minimize the evil in their desires, they must begin by accepting a crucial and fundamental truth: desires should be servants and not lords. Desires can help us to do the things we ought to do; we should never allow them to usurp the place of the law of God and the Spirit of God and become the criterion of our conduct.

What is a Christian's criterion of conduct? Jesus sums up the law in the two great commandments: love God and love your neighbor (Mk 12:28-34). The apostle Paul similarly states that love is the fulfillment of the law (Rom 13:8-10; Gal 5:14). A Christian is to be guided by love rather than by his desires.

That statement may seem like a contradiction, for "Is not love itself a type of desire?" It is certainly true that the Greek word *eros* has to do with desire, but that is not the case with *agape,* the key New Testament word for love. The love that guides Christian conduct is not a desire or an emotion. Instead, it is a commitment to serve others, to put others first, to lay down our lives for others, even as Jesus laid down his life for us (Jn 13:12-17, 34-35; 15:12-13; Gal 5:13; Eph 5:2; 1 Jn 3:16-18). This is the standard of Christian conduct—the law of love lived out in the Spirit of love. Our desires are servants to help us live fully in the love of Christ.

Of course, in a certain sense the change occurs in response to an external force—the revelation of God's desires. However, this external force produces a genuine internal change when we respond to it sincerely from the heart and in the power of the indwelling Holy Spirit.

Christians should expect their desires to change as they learn to live more and more for the Lord. In my own life I can see that my righteous desires are much stronger and my unrighteous ones much weaker today than they were when I first became a Christian in my college days. On occasion, unrighteous and unruly desires still raise their heads. Some of them will probably accompany me to the end of my earthly life. Nonetheless, significant change has occurred, and more will occur in the future. The Lord will help our desires to change so that we can serve him in greater freedom.

## Love God

Pastoral leaders can help fellow Christians take several steps that will facilitate a positive change in their desires. The first step is to set one's heart on the Lord himself, on loving him and his ways, on growing in a personal relationship with him.

For many Christians God is a distant and impersonal force who must be served and obeyed dutifully but who can never be really *known*. In scripture, to know God is to encounter him personally, to experience his goodness and his power and his holiness—"to know the love of Christ which surpasses knowledge" (Eph 3:19). This type of knowledge cannot be separated from love and faith. When we know the Lord in this way, our obedience to him ceases to be a dutiful gesture of homage to a remote deity and becomes instead an expression of a loving personal relationship with a Father who is king of the universe. As Jesus said, "If you love me, you will keep my commandments" (Jn 14:15, 21, 23; 15:10).

Loving obedience such as this leads a Christian not only to desire to do God's will, but even to desire what God desires. It leads one to respond readily and eagerly to his word, to "run in the way" of his commands (Ps 119:32). An earnest desire to please him should grow to the point where it overwhelms all contrary desires and holds them captive.

In a similar way Christians can reorient their desires toward loving other people. Some Christians interpret *agape* as the sort of dry, detached, impersonal service that would allow one to say, "Oh yes, I love Fred, but I'll never like the man." This attitude invites conflicting desires. Instead, we should set our heart on *knowing* others as well as serving them, laying down our lives for others within a loving personal relationship, even as Jesus gave his life out of a genuine committed personal love (Jn 13:1). Christians should actively cultivate relationships with those the Lord calls them to love. Then they will find that their desires increasingly support them in living a life of committed love.

## *Surrender*

A second step that will help people reorient their desires is to surrender to God's will completely and from the heart. Conflict between God's desires and ours sometimes indicates that we still hold a tight grip on certain areas of our life: we are unwilling to abandon ourselves totally to God.

For example, I once experienced a strong and undisciplined desire to engage in a particular form of Christian work. The desire seemed to be from the Lord, but it was not yet time for it to be realized. I found it very difficult to submit to God's will in the matter and desire what he desired—which was to defer my calling till a future date, to be revealed by him in his good pleasure. As I prayed about the matter, I began to see my true condition—I had not really surrendered the entire area to him. I wanted to serve the Lord, but I wanted to do it *my* way and in *my* timing. As I repented for my lack of abandonment, I found a new freedom to accept God's will with joy and even to desire what he desired.

Why do Christians hold on to things rather than surrendering them to God? Often the reason lies in a lack of trust. In my own case, I feared that I would lose precious years of my life and be less fruitful once I turned my hands to the task. I felt as if *I* needed to act to preserve the potential fruitfulness of my service. How absurd! Couldn't I trust God to provide the fruit at the proper time? My part is to focus on doing whatever he calls me to do when he calls me to do it.

God is all-powerful, all-knowing, and all-loving. Pastoral leaders should teach people they can trust that the direction God gives them will be for their own good and for the good of his kingdom. One who trusts totally in God can surrender himself more freely to his will; one who surrenders to his will can more readily desire the things he desires.

At this point it is important to distinguish desires from compulsions and addictions. For various reasons desires can develop into compulsions—habitual actions that are extremely difficult to overcome. To bring about a change, the person must repent from the heart. But there may also be the need for deliverance from spiritual bondage, and then for help gradually to reverse the pattern. The pastoral leader must distinguish between the case in which the person has not fundamentally decided to renounce the desire from the case in which the person has made the renunciation but needs further help.

This distinction must be made in helping someone with an actual addiction, such as alcohol. A complicating factor where addiction is involved is that physical craving may have replaced any other desire, and the person may actually have come to detest what he also continues to desire.

## Be Honest

A third step in reorienting desires is honesty. All Christians experience some wayward desires which conflict with God's will. An honest acknowledgment of wrong desires will lead to a greater progress in learning to live with them and even in changing them.

The greatest obstacle to honesty about desires is false shame. People are sometimes ashamed of what they desire, and therefore try to hide it. Many people would feel some embarrassment at admitting that they do certain things to impress people and be the center of attention, or admitting that they have lied, or that they have a desire to quit everything and travel around the world. Often people are especially ashamed of their sexual desires.

Shame is the right response to sinful behavior. Adam and Eve naturally felt shame for their guilt, as illustrated by their sudden sense of nakedness (Gn 2:25; 3:7, 10). However, shame is not the right response to desires. Often, wayward desires are only temptations to sin rather than sin itself. Often, they are merely natural human desires that are inappropriate in the given situation. Christians should be discreet and modest in acknowledging desires, but they should not be ashamed.

To whom should people honestly acknowledge their desires? First, Christians should be honest with themselves. Rather than either rationalizing or repressing their desires, they should face up to them and acknowledge them for what they are.

Second, they should be honest with the Lord. Rather than waiting for their desires to change before speaking to the Lord about them, they should present their unruly desires before him, admitting them openly in prayer, and seeking help from him in managing and even changing them.

Third, they should be honest with a brother or sister in Christ. Rather than keeping their desires simply between themselves and God, they should acknowledge them before a trusted counselor, eagerly receiving the advice or support they might give. Those who honestly acknowledge their desires to themselves, the Lord, and another person will grow in self-control and even see their desires change.

Pastoral leaders facilitate honesty by hearing people out when they wish to discuss embarrassing desires and not cutting them off with a hasty admonition. Often the pastoral leader can arrange for the person to become part of a support group. Sometimes this can prove more beneficial to the person than if the pastoral leader worked directly with him or her.

In other cases a person can be helped by an intensive pastoral effort. To get control of a particular desire, a person might profit from having some one person to talk with regularly who offers help, not simply correction. The two can make an agreement that the one being helped will tell the other when he fails to do what is right; the other can offer frequent counsel and prayer.

## Discipline

A fourth step in reorienting desires is to work for change. Christians can gradually master many of their errant desires through the prudent exercise of discipline and self-denial. As with emotions in general, desires can be compared to children.

Sometimes the right way to help a child is to show patience and forbearance; at other times it is better to discipline the child and resist his or her stubborn and rebellious will. In similar fashion it is sometimes helpful to bring our desires into submission through force. A persistent refusal to yield to desires weakens them and increases one's control.

Sometimes it is helpful to decide to deliberately ignore a desire. For instance, a Christian who is fasting one day walks past a bakery. Smelling the aroma of fresh baked goods, he lingers in front of the window. After a few minutes he gets a hold of himself and walks away. He says to himself, "All right, if I'm going to be like that, I'll fast another day. I'm not going to let my body get away with that."

Sometimes one can grow in mastery of desires in one area by disciplining desires in another area. For example, many Christians of the past found that fasting can help control sexual desire. Desires are interconnected with one another in such a way that a whole cluster of desires can change in response to a strong tug on one or two of them.

It is important to help the person we are guiding to determine whether a problem with desires stems from too much or too little control. Some people are *very* controlled. To encourage them to fast in order to overcome problems with their desires will only cause them to be anxious and overscrupulous. Other people lack control in much of their lives. They do not know how to say no to themselves. It is helpful for them to pick one simple area, to decide to control it, and to get it into shape. They might start with almost anything—eating, television watching, impulsive buying.

Working to change desires is not the most important step in reorienting them. Setting one's heart on the Lord, surrendering to his will, and honestly acknowledging one's desires are all of greater importance. Nonetheless, working for change is also very helpful. Just as Paul worked to pummel his body and subdue it (1 Cor 9:27), so Christians should work to subdue their desires and bring them under the reign of Christ.

## Impart Confidence

Finally, I would offer the following pastoral observations.

First, it is often helpful to encourage people struggling with unruly and sinful desires not to take their desires too seriously. Usually people are capable of doing the right thing even when their desires oppose them. A person may feel tired, depressed, and unenthusiastic about prayer, but he or she can still choose to pray. Better to pray and forget about contrary inclinations than to fret introspectively about one's irreligious desires and never actually come before the Lord.

We should help people learn to deal confidently with their disorderly desires. Several years ago I counseled a young man who experienced strong perverse sexual attractions. As long as he was anxious about these desires and terrified of yielding to them, he made little progress. The breakthrough came when he realized that his anxiety was more of a problem than his desires. As he grew more confident and peaceful about dealing with the disorder, the disorder itself began to wane.

## Internal Data

Second, when we are helping someone make a decision, we should teach them to pay some attention to morally neutral and positive desires. Christians should regard their inclinations as data to be taken into account with all the other relevant data. A desire for something can be a stroke in its favor, for desire helps a person act with greater zeal and vigor. For example, most people perform more successfully at a job they like than at one they dislike. Therefore, desire for a particular job is a relevant piece of data.

However, desire is not the only consideration to be taken account of, nor even the most important. For example, taking again the example of a job decision, other data exceed in importance the question of desire. For example, a person should ask, will this job enable me to provide adequate financial support for my family? Will the job allow me to spend enough time with my family and church? Does the company employ unrighteous methods in its work, or is there anything pronouncedly anti-Christian in the company's goals or work environment? Has the Lord given any other indications of what his mind might be? The answers to these questions should form the final decision more than the person's desires, though their desires should also be taken into account.

## Desires without Ability

The third pastoral observation also concerns people's neutral and positive desires. While many pastoral leaders are at least sometimes willing to steer people away from wrong or clearly inappropriate desires, they are very reluctant to offer advice that discourages people from following good desires. Few pastors would try to dissuade a young man from pursuing a legitimate career which he strongly desires—as Randy's pastor did when he recommended that Randy leave medicine for pastoral ministry. We too seldom question whether a person's desires are in fact matched by gifts. Many Christians have good desires, such as wanting to go into full-time Christian work, to be a missionary, to be a minister or priest. But we know from experience that not everyone who feels thus is called. A person might have pure and holy desires for certain kinds of service, but simply not have the capacity. Or, as in Randy's case, a person may have many abilities but may most desire to labor in an area where the Lord is not calling him or her. In either case, people might profit from the counsel of a more mature, experienced Christian who can help them sort out their desires and God's call. Without pressuring people, there is a place in pastoral ministry for advising people to put aside good desires, either to avoid taking a mistaken path or for the sake of the greater glory of God.

If, in response to such counsel, a person freely and from the heart chooses to go against his or her strongest desire, he or she can expect the decision to be followed eventually by a shift in desires. Randy made his choice several years ago. It is clear to him now that he made the right decision. In retrospect he sees the value of the gifts and abilities he has as an evangelist and pastor. His desires have changed. He would not want to be doing anything other than what he is doing now.

In conclusion, desires are a gift from God, a part of human makeup that has a proper role and function. Desires can easily get Christians into trouble, but they can also be an aid in loving and serving the Lord. God's intention is not to root them out, but to work in Christians' lives so that more and more they desire what he desires.

# FOUR

# True and False Humility

IF THE PEOPLE YOU PASTOR are like those I pastor, one of their common problems is feeling bad about themselves. The reasons vary—guilt, insecurity, even self-hatred.

One cause of low self-esteem is particularly tricky to deal with because it seems so like a Christian virtue. I am referring to the problem of poor self-image that masquerades as humility. Many Christians think that humility consists of feeling bad about themselves. In effect they believe that they are supposed to have a poor self-image.

Because of this misconception, many Christians have an extra obstacle in the way of a healthy self-image. Like the rest of the people in our society they inherit a general tendency toward a bad self-image. But, in addition, they hold a view that idealizes the very patterns they should be fighting. So any attempt to help Christians overcome self-image problems has to distinguish between true and false humility.

According to the "humility equals self-denigration" school of thought, the humble man speaks of himself as follows: "I'm wretched, useless, worthless, despicable, and vile." He speaks and thinks about his abilities, his character, and his worth in a way that asserts his basic human poverty.

C.S. Lewis gets to the heart of the problem with this view of humility in one of his Screwtape letters. The fictional author of the *Screwtape Letters* is a senior tempter in hell, who is writing to a junior demon in order to pass on important advice in the art of deception.

You must therefore conceal from the patient the true end of humility. Let him think of it not as self-forgetfulness but as a certain kind of opinion (namely, a low opinion) of his own talents and character. Some talents, I gather, he really has. Fix in his mind the idea that humility consists in trying to believe those talents to be less valuable than he believes them to be. No doubt they are less valuable than he believes, but that is not the point. The great thing is to make him value an opinion for some quality other than truth, thus introducing an element of dishonesty and make-believe into the heart of what otherwise threatens to become a virtue. By this method thousands of humans have been brought to think that humility means pretty women trying to believe they are ugly and clever men trying to believe they are fools. And since what they are trying to believe may, in some cases, be manifest nonsense, they cannot succeed in believing it, and we have the chance of keeping their minds endlessly revolving on themselves in an effort to achieve the impossible.

The chief fallacy in this interpretation of humility, says Lewis (through the mouth of Screwtape), is that it places little value on gaining a truthful and accurate perception of oneself. Rather it encourages one to adopt the lowest possible view of oneself, regardless of truth. The outcome is a self-centered mental effort doomed to end in introspection and frustration.

## Sober Self-Appraisal

The scriptural teaching on how Christians should look at themselves is found in the twelfth chapter of Romans: "For by the grace given to me I bid every one among you not to think of himself more highly than he ought to think, but to *think with sober judgment,* each according to the measure of faith which God has assigned him" (Rom 12:3).

Paul teaches that Christians should hold an opinion of

themselves based on "sober judgment." The Greek word used here could also be translated as "clear-mindedness," "reasonableness," "sensibleness," or "moderation." To think with sober judgment is to think accurately, truthfully, without veering off to unjustified extremes. God wants Christians to hold as *truthful* an opinion of themselves as possible, not as *low* an opinion as possible.

The opposite of sober self-appraisal is exhibited vividly in people who are intoxicated with alcohol. They tend to view themselves according to two different extremes. Either their self-image becomes inflated until they see themselves as witty, powerful, and irresistibly attractive, or their self-image gets punctured and they fall into a state of melancholy, depression, and self-pity. In either case their self-image is a gross caricature of reality. Sober judgment is lost as the intoxicated person becomes, in his own eyes, a dashing hero or a debased, unlovable monster.

Christian teaching about self-image avoids both of these extremes. The Christian view is based on truth, not on "dishonesty and make-believe" (as Screwtape would have it).

How does one find out this truth about oneself? Some truths are particular to us as individuals: for example, our own unique constellation of strengths and weaknesses. To get at these truths, a Christian needs the assistance of someone outside himself. This is one important function of parents and pastors; those who are older, wiser, and in a position of responsibility are often in the best position to tell us the truth about ourselves.

However, some truths about ourselves as human beings and as Christians apply to all of us. Two sets of truths are especially important.

The first set teaches us about the importance of subordination to and dependence upon God and our fellow human beings. Human beings are not autonomous, self-sufficient units. They are creatures made by God, dependent upon him for natural and spiritual life, and created to be interdependent with other human beings. Furthermore, the world does not revolve around any one of us. There is no human being who is indispensable to God's plan. We need to fit in with his plans and purposes; he does not have to fit in with ours. Understanding this basic truth can go a long way toward preventing an inflated self-image.

The second set of truths complement the first. Though we are not independent of God or indispensable to him, he does love us, value us, and treat us as one of the most important parts of his vast creation. He created us in his own image and likeness. He sent his Son, the eternal Word through whom everything was made, to become a human being and live among us. Though marred by sin, we were still valuable enough in his sight for him to purchase us "not with perishable things such as silver or gold, but with the precious blood of Christ" (1 Pt 1:18-19). He has also given each of us gifts that we might serve him and help to advance his kingdom in the world.

In light of this, it is a mistake for someone to maintain an excessively low self-evaluation. If God does not hold such an opinion of us, then we should not hold it of ourselves. God certainly wants to destroy our self-concern, self-protectiveness, and stubborn, independent pride, but he also wants us to know our proper worth in his sight. Again, C.S. Lewis puts it best, speaking through Screwtape:

> To anticipate the Enemy's strategy, we must consider his aims. . . . He wants each man, in the long run, to be able to recognize all creatures (even himself) as glorious and excellent things. He wants to kill their animal self-love as soon as possible; but it is his long-term policy, I fear, to restore to them a new kind of self-love—a charity and gratitude for all selves, including their own. . . . For we must never forget what is the most repellent and inexplicable trait in our Enemy; he really loves the hairless bipeds he has created, and always gives back to them with his right hand what he has taken away with his left.

## Humility as Timidity

Mistaking humility for low self-esteem is sometimes complicated by a further mistake. Some Christians misunderstand humility, thinking that it refers to reserved, unassertive behavior. This misunderstanding often covers up a problem of timidity, a weakness usually connected to emotional insecurity and a poor self-image; it also keeps people from serving the Lord effectively and confidently.

I once asked a young man in our community to assist regularly with music at our worship services. He was exceptionally gifted in music and was very able to lead others in worship. But he responded to my request with great reluctance.

"Such a position of prominence might keep me from being humble," he replied. As we talked further, I became convinced that he had a problem with timidity supported by a false view of humility. He finally chose to accept the assignment, and his new service helped him to grow in confidence and boldness.

## Humble Boldness

Scripture is full of exhortations to confidence and boldness, and equally full of examples of men and women who exhibited just these qualities. The classic text on timidity is found in 2 Timothy: "Hence I remind you to rekindle the gift of God that is within you through the laying on of my hands; for God did not give us a spirit of timidity but a spirit of power and love and self-control. Do not be ashamed then of testifying to our Lord, nor to me his prisoner, but share in suffering for the gospel in the power of God" (1:6-8).

Paul exhorts Timothy to stir up the gift he received when he had been ordained for his ministry in Ephesus. Timothy is not to be timid or afraid, for the Spirit he has received from God— the Holy Spirit—is not a spirit of timidity, but of power and love and self-control.

All of the great men and women presented in scripture act

with courage, confidence, and boldness. Moses marching up to Pharaoh, David engaging Goliath in battle, Esther pleading for the life of her people, Jeremiah and Ezekiel prophesying to rebellious Judah, Jesus cleansing the temple and chastising the Jewish leaders, Paul rebuking the Galatians—all are examples of men and women who were able to act aggressively, decisively, and confidently in conformity to the will of God. Humility does not mean being shy or timid.

## *Servanthood*

If we are to counter these harmful misunderstandings of humility, we must teach people the true meaning of Christian humility. The key New Testament passage on humility is found in Philippians:

> Do nothing from selfishness or conceit, but in humility count others better than yourselves. Let each of you look not only to his own interests, but also to the interests of others. Have this mind among yourselves, which is yours in Christ Jesus, who, though he was in the form of God, did not count equality with God a thing to be grasped, but emptied himself, taking the form of a servant, being born in the likeness of men. And being found in human form he humbled himself and became obedient unto death, even death on a cross. Therefore God has highly exalted him and bestowed on him the name which is above every name, that at the name of Jesus every knee should bow, in heaven and on earth and under the earth, and every tongue confess that Jesus Christ is Lord, to the glory of God the Father. (2:3-11)

Perhaps the potentially most misleading statement in this passage is the second half of verse three: "In humility count others better than yourselves." According to the modern understanding of the word "better" one could take this verse to mean that a humble Christian should think of everyone as superior to himself in value, ability, and virtue. This interpretation would support the view that Christian humility means having a low opinion of oneself.

Contemporary English has almost lost the meaning of the word "better" which is important for understanding this passage. The word referred to those in a higher social position. One's "betters" were those "above" one in the accepted structure of society, those whom one would honor in a special way. The term was used especially of those whom servants served.

The command "Count others better than yourselves" could thus be accurately restated, "Be a servant to others." The servant regards himself as responsible for the needs and interests of those over him. He is at the disposal of others. He is not able to order his life according to his own preferences, but must subordinate his ambitions, his decisions, his entire life to the needs and concerns of those he is serving. To regard others as "better" than ourselves means that we count others as people whom we are obligated to honor, attend to, and serve. In fact, the best commentary on the meaning of verse three is the verse that follows it: "Let each of you look not only to his own interests, but also to the interests of others."

The opposites of humility are "selfishness" and "conceit" (verse 3). The Greek word for "selfishness" could also be translated as "self-seeking" or "selfish ambition." The selfish man is out to advance himself and his position without regard to the needs or interests of others. The Greek word for "conceit" could be translated more literally as "empty glory" or "vainglory." To act from empty glory is to seek honor, attention, and admiration from others. Both selfishness and conceit are forms of self-concern and self-service. They are opposed to Christian humility, the characteristic of one who is a servant to others.

## The Perfect Model

The passage in Philippians then proceeds to describe the perfect model of humility—Jesus Christ, the Son of God. Jesus "humbled himself, taking the form of a servant." He did not cling to his divine privileges, but lowered himself, walking among us as a mere man, suffering shame, humiliation, and death on our behalf. Jesus is the perfect example of humility: the man who is truly a servant, who looks not only to his own interests, but to the interests of others.

Jesus did not hold a low opinion of himself. He knew he was the Son of God, the Messiah, the Holy One of Israel. Neither was he timid or reserved in demeanor. He was able to be silent when necessary, but he spoke freely when it was appropriate to speak. He was bold, decisive, able to take initiative and to act with daring. Though he did not allow a concern for his own honor and position to prevent him from fulfilling his mission on earth, he was able to receive honor from his Father when the Father "highly exalted him and bestowed on him the name which is above every name." Thus we see in Jesus a man free from false humility and full of true humility.

## A Modern Affliction

While an accurate understanding of the scripture regarding self-evaluation, boldness, and true humility can help clear up some of the reasons why Christians' feel bad about themselves, scripture does not present an explicit approach to the problem. It does not speak directly about how to overcome a poor self-image. Why not, we might ask. After all, this is such a common problem.

The main reasons are historical and social. Every society has its own unique set of challenges and problems. People in first-century Palestine, fifth-century North Africa, thirteenth-century Byzantium, and eighteenth-century Germany had their own distinct circumstances, and these presented certain obstacles to living the Christian life. In twentieth-century America we face many unprecedented social and psychological problems as a consequence of the development of technological society. Divorce, suicide, drug and alcohol addictions, psychological breakdown all afflict us to a greater degree than they have afflicted other societies in the past. Problems with self-image fall into this same category. Contemporary society affects people in such a way that low self-esteem is a particularly common problem. This difficulty affects Americans today in a way that it did not affect people in the cultures of Moses, David, Jesus, or Paul.

Though scripture does not try to anticipate all the problems that will be encountered by different human societies, it does teach a set of principles that can be applied effectively to any human situation. From scripture we can learn important wisdom about how to overcome problems with a poor self-image. The following recommendations for helping people develop a positive self-image are based on scriptural principles.

## Developing a Positive Self-Image

First, acknowledge the problem. Scripture teaches us to correct our subjective opinions with objective truth. Doubts, fears, and discouragement are best dealt with by embracing the truth.

The primary obstacle to a positive self-image for many people stems from the fact that they give full credence to their bad feelings about themselves. They are convinced that their discouragement and depression come from the fact that they *are* worthless and unloved. In fact they are depressed because they *feel* they are worthless and unloved. They need to acknowledge their true problem—the problem is not with their selves but with how they *see* themselves. They suffer from a self-image problem.

Second, repent of bad attitudes. The scriptural solution to distorted views of ourselves is *metanoia,* a change of mind. This means that people should repent for believing lies about themselves. They should learn to distinguish the lies from the truth, and learn to reject the lies.

They should also repent for self-pity and self-preoccupation. People with a poor self-image often get lost in introspectiveness, worrying about themselves, pitying themselves, wondering what others think of them. This pattern is difficult to break. A person must start by recognizing the pattern for what it is and deciding that it ought to change.

Third, believe the truth. Christians need to embrace the foundational scriptural truths about who they are: men and women created in the image of God, of precious value to him, redeemed from sin by the blood of Jesus Christ, gifted by the Holy Spirit. They also need to receive positive, accurate evaluation from brothers and sisters in Christ, and regard it more highly than their own slanted, negative judgment.

Fourth, receive encouragement. People who suffer from a poor self-image cannot change their self-image by themselves. They need the help of others. In particular, they need supportive relationships that provide encouragement, affection, and Christian love. They need the life of the body of Christ.

As pastoral leaders we need to take special responsibility to see that such relationships exist among our people. However, we must also urge our people to take proper initiative in building these relationships. People with self-image problems often tend to be afraid of others and to keep to themselves. They must learn how to reach out to other people and establish relationships that provide a channel for growth.

Fifth, serve in humility. The positive side of repentance for accepting lies about oneself is to believe the truth. The positive side of repentance for self-pity and self-preoccupation is to serve humbly. People with self-image problems need to learn how to reach out to other people not only so that their own needs will be met but also so that they can meet the needs of others. In fact, forgetting about their own problems and concentrating instead on caring for others is an important step in overcoming these problems. False humility is a conniving accomplice of self-image problems, but true humility helps to overcome them.

Sixth, fight with perseverance. Fighting problems with self-image is not like fighting a boxer with a glass jaw who can be knocked out in the first round. These problems are usually tough opponents, holding their ground tenaciously, giving way only after a drawn-out contest. Therefore, patience and perseverance are essential components of victory.

The need for perseverance is especially crucial for people dealing with a poor self-image because the problem often leads to discouragement in the face of obstacles. So such people are very likely to grow discouraged trying to overcome the problem itself. People who are fighting a poor self-image will probably need help in this very area.

Seventh, pray with faith. People with self-image problems need help not only from their brothers and sisters in the Lord, but also directly from the Lord himself. As usual, the Lord is ready to aid his people. Seeking the Lord with faith can bring great advances in overcoming self-image problems. Nothing can substitute for a strong relationship with the Lord, in which his power is released in the life of the believer.

# FIVE

# Not Guilty!

M ANY CHRISTIANS TODAY LABOR under a ponderous burden of self-condemnation. This burden weighs them down spiritually and emotionally, often plunging them into self-pity, discouragement, and depression.

Other Christians, inspired by secular currents of thought, deny basic tenets of traditional Christian morality, opting instead for a more flexible and up-to-date ethical system. One is free to break the Ten Commandments if one's motives are pure.

Obviously, neither of these approaches embody the way the Lord intended the Christian life to be lived.

Today, pastoral leaders face the challenge of liberating people from self-condemnation without diluting the demands of the gospel. Christ calls his people to a life of peace with God and a life of holiness. The Lord wants a people both irreproachable in his sight and unshackled by habitual self-reproach. Here, as in so many other areas, the Christian pastor faces a difficult task.

## Guilt as Feeling

Christians in Western society often fall prey to one of two defective approaches to guilt. These approaches offer a distorted analysis of what guilt is and how it should be responded to. Those who take the first approach are subjectivizers, and those who take the second approach are idealizers.

According to the view most common in contemporary society, guilt is a subjective emotional state. A recent author defined guilt in the following manner: "Let us tentatively define guilt as a feeling that we have done or felt something unacceptable to someone."[8] We should notice two important features of this definition. First, guilt is defined as a feeling. It is not an objective condition that follows upon the violation of God's commands but a subjective emotional state that can be examined and corrected independent of absolute moral criteria. Second, guilt arises when we feel that we have displeased other people, not when we have done something morally objectionable. The objective moral categories of right and wrong are excluded from this definition and replaced by the more neutral, relative, and subjective phrase "unacceptable to someone."

The practical consequence of this approach to guilt is that therapists and counselors often focus predominantly or exclusively on alleviating dysfunctional feelings of guilt among their clients while ignoring any objective guilt that may exist. Guilt is considered a subjective psychological phenomenon that can be eliminated through strictly psychological techniques. Christian counselors are sometimes influenced by this approach, and thereby lose a clear perception of the biblical teaching on righteousness and holiness.

## Guilt as an Ideal

The second defective approach to guilt is a distinctively Christian invention. In some ways it is the opposite of the subjectivist approach. Whereas the subjectivizers tend to view guilt feelings as dysfunctional and in need of eradication, the idealizers embrace a poignant conviction of guilt as a sign of progress in holiness.

Since we cannot draw near to the perfect and holy God without simultaneously recognizing our imperfection and impurity—so the reasoning goes—the Christian ideal summons us to meditate continually upon our wickedness and corruption. This is the best spiritual antidote to pride and vainglory. The more we feel our moral failures, the more we have grown in virtue.

An idealized approach to guilt feelings is certainly less distorted and damaging than the approach proposed by the subjectivizers. It can even be found in the writings of many great Christians of the past. In former centuries the idealized view of guilt feelings does not appear to have fostered an emotional problem with self-condemnation. In fact, it may even have helped some people live a virtuous and committed Christian life.

However, in today's society this approach has more unfortunate consequences. Characterized by widespread family breakdown, an unstable and impersonal technological social system, and a general state of alienation, our society subjects individuals to extremes of emotional stress which often produce problems with insecurity, anxiety, and self-hatred. In this social context a lack of balance in the Christian understanding of guilt can cause severe psychological hardship.

## *Guilt as Fact*

Scripture teaches much about guilt. The errors in subjectivizing and idealizing guilt become evident as we study the biblical teaching. In contrast to these two approaches, scripture asserts the objectivity of guilt and the ideal of a clear conscience.

In scripture, guilt is an objective condition and not a subjective emotional state. In fact, in some passages of Leviticus the word translated "guilt" is applied particularly to unintentional and unknown sins: "If the whole congregation of Israel commits a sin unwittingly and the thing is hidden from the eyes of the assembly, and they do any one of the things which the Lord has commanded not be done *and are guilty*; when the sin which they have committed becomes known, the assembly shall offer a young bull for a sin offering and bring it before the tent of meeting (Lv 4:13-14; see also Lv 4:22-24, 27-28, 5:1-2, 6:1-7).

The assembly here is said to be guilty of the sin before they have even become aware of the act. In this passage guilt is an objective condition which follows upon the violation of God's commandments; it is totally independent of one's emotional and psychological state. This understanding is consistent with the older dictionary definition of the English word guilt: "the *fact* of having committed a breach of conduct, especially violating law and involving a penalty."

The biblical approach to guilt presumes the existence of an objective moral law. According to scripture, God has issued a moral law that is eternal and absolute, not historically and culturally relative (Mt 5:17-20; Rom 3:31, 8:4-8, 13:6-10); we can all know this moral law, for God has clearly revealed it (Dt 30:11-14; Is 2:14; Rom 2:14-16); God holds all human beings accountable for their faithlessness and disobedience to his word (Mt 7:24-27; Rom 2:6-11; 1 Cor 6:9-10; 2 Cor 5:10; Heb 2:1-4, 10:26-31; Jas 2:8-13).

## Repairing the Wrong

Since God's fundamental moral law is objective, eternal, absolute, and knowable, those who violate this law bear an objective burden of guilt, whether they stumble sorrowfully under the load or bear it in ignorance or calculated rebellion.

According to the biblical notion of guilt, a guilty man is at odds with the Lord. He has ruptured his relationship with God. If he is to be at peace with God again, the wrong must be made right. It is not enough to therapeutically assuage his painful feelings of guilt; a broken relationship must be repaired.

Neither is it enough to simply allow time to heal the relationship. Human beings may forget wrongdoing with the passing of time, but God does not forget. He is gracious and ready to forgive, but the objective guilt must be removed through objective means.

Scripture illustrates this truth. Leviticus 4-6 states three of the requirements God imposed on Israelites who were guilty of sin and desired reconciliation: confession (5:5), restitution (6:1-5), and sacrifice (6:6-7, and chapters 4 and 5).

These particular objective requirements apply to the New Covenant as well as to the Old. The atoning work of Christ becomes our efficacious offering, but it does not eliminate the need for confession and restitution—in a word, repentance.

Scripture, therefore, teaches that guilt is an objective condition and not merely a subjective emotional state. As an objective condition it can only be removed by objective means—sacrifice and repentance. Scripture knows nothing of a subjectivized notion of guilt.

The biblical teaching also conflicts with the approach of the idealizers. Scripture does not exhort us to idealize feelings of guilt, moral failure, and personal inadequacy. We are not beckoned to a life of self-reproach and moral discontent. Instead, scripture calls us to live with a clear conscience, confident of our right standing with the Lord.

One of the best examples in scripture of a man with a clear conscience is the apostle Paul. Many people infer from Paul's theology that he suffered from a morbid and tormented sense of personal sin, but all the evidence contradicts this view. Rather, we see a man confident that he was living in basic conformity to God's purpose for his life.

> And Paul, looking intently at the council, said, "Brethren, I have lived before God in all good conscience up to this day." (Acts 23:1)

> For our boast is this, the testimony of our conscience that we have behaved in the world, and still more toward you, with holiness and godly sincerity, not by earthly wisdom but by the grace of God." (2 Cor 1:12)

> You are witnesses, and God also, how holy and righteous and blameless was our behavior to you believers."
> (1 Thes 2:10)

Paul asserts confidently that he has behaved righteously before God and man. This confidence is echoed by the author of the Letter to the Hebrews: "Pray for us, for we are sure that we have a clear conscience, desiring to act honorably in all things (Heb 13:18).

The apostles do not apologize for their sinful inadequacy, as we might expect. On the contrary, they proclaim loudly that their consciences are clear. Paul's clear conscience does not lead him to arrogance or presumption. Though his conscience testifies to his right conduct, he acknowledges that the final verdict belongs to God. *"I am not aware of anything against myself, but I am not thereby acquitted. It is the Lord who judges me.* Therefore do not pronounce judgment before the time, before the Lord comes, who will bring to light the things now hidden in darkness and will disclose the purposes of the heart" (1 Cor 4:4-5).

The Greek verb translated here as "I am not aware" is the root from which the Greek noun for "conscience" is derived. Paul thus asserts again that his conscience is clear: "I am not aware of anything against myself." However, he also recognizes that only the Lord knows "the things now hidden in darkness" and "the purposes of the heart." With him stands the final judgment.

There are two titles that Paul assigns himself which on first reading appear to deny that his conscience is clear. He calls himself "the foremost of sinners" (1 Tm 1:15) and "least of the apostles" (1 Cor 15:9).

However, Paul is not bewailing his continual propensity to sin; he has something very specific in mind. In both passages Paul is speaking of his former persecution of the church: "though I formerly blasphemed and persecuted and insulted him" (1 Tm 1:13); "because I persecuted the church of God" (1 Cor 15:9). Paul had committed an objectively grave sin, and he freely confesses this fact. Nonetheless, God has saved him in Christ and given him the grace to live a life that is "holy and righteous and blameless" (1 Thes 2:10).

The apostle Paul had a clear conscience, and the author of the Letter to the Hebrews had a clear conscience. According to the biblical teaching, this clarity of conscience is not a lofty ideal unobtainable by the rank and file of the saints. It is meant for all Christians:

The aim of our charge is love that issues from a pure heart and a good conscience and sincere faith. (1 Tm 1:5)

Wage the good warfare, holding faith and a good conscience.
(1 Tm 1:18-19)

Keep your conscience clear, so that, when you are abused, those who revile your good behavior in Christ may be put to shame. (1 Pt 3:16)

The biblical teaching thus corrects the distortions and excesses of both the subjectivizers and the idealizers. It teaches us that guilt is an objective condition and not merely a subjective emotion. It also teaches us that the Christian ideal is a clear conscience and not shame and self-reproach. These are important and powerful truths that should shape the way we pastor our people.

## Contrition

Many Christians fail to believe that they can have a clear conscience, because they misunderstand some related concepts. In particular, many confuse contrition with condemnation and basic righteousness with flawlessness. The first step in helping people overcome self-condemnation is to clarify these concepts and thereby press home the ideal of a clear conscience.

Contrition is a word which means sorrow for sin. "The sacrifice acceptable to God is a broken spirit; a broken and a contrite heart, O God, thou wilt not despise" (Ps 51:17). Contrition is an important element in the process of turning from wrongdoing to righteousness. As such, Christians have always prized it highly.

Many Christians today confuse contrition with self-condemnation, but the two are actually quite different. Contrition derives from a concern for an offended party—God, and perhaps one of our fellow human beings—and also from a concern for our relationship with them. We grieve because they have been wronged through our conduct and because our relationship with them has been damaged.

Self-condemnation, on the other hand, derives from self-concern. We condemn ourselves because we have failed to match up to our own personal standards and because our low self-evaluation has been confirmed by our conduct.

Contrition leads to a positive change in behavior. Paul states this clearly in 2 Corinthians 7:9-11: "I rejoice . . . because you were grieved into repenting. . . . For godly grief produces a repentance that leads to salvation and brings no regret, but worldly grief produces death." Contrition is an aspect of repentance leading us along the road to righteousness.

Self-condemnation, on the other hand, leads to self-hatred, discouragement, depression, and self-pity. Instead of issuing in a positive behavioral change, self-condemnation actually impedes such a change. Like "worldly grief," self-condemnation "produces death."

Pastoral leaders must grow adept at distinguishing between self-condemnation and contrition and at helping others make the same distinction. Christians can never overcome a problem with self-condemnation if they are idealizing the problem—considering it a virtue.

## An Overscrupulous Response

Once Christians grasp the importance of living righteously, they sometimes begin to see wrongdoing in every nook and cranny of their life. This response especially characterizes those who suffer from a problem with self-condemnation. Every small flaw gets magnified into a major sin, blocking a peaceful relationship with God and tarnishing a sensitive conscience. Though it looks like commendable zeal for righteousness, these types of moral scruples can actually lead to frustration, discouragement, and consequent negligence in matters of far greater spiritual import.

Such misguided zeal sometimes leads Christians to evaluate as morally wrong things that are in fact only regrettable. So, for example, many take too seriously temptations of thought or emotion, mistakes, performance failures, and personal weaknesses. These features of life are an inevitable aspect of frail humanity living in a fallen creation. They will not depart from us until we receive our resurrected bodies in the new heaven and new earth. We should regret and attempt to limit their intrusion into our lives, but we should not allow them to stain our consciences.

Being overscrupulous can also lead Christians to exaggerate small faults and to relate to them as major sins. We certainly should not ignore small faults; the Lord wants to change us and remove many of these defects, though they may be slight. Nevertheless, the fact that we tend to talk too much (or too little) and often forget to call mother on her birthday should not make us feel that our relationship with the Lord is in serious disrepair. We can have small faults and still live with a clear conscience, so long as we are peacefully and persistently seeking to change.

One of the greatest responsibilities of a pastoral counselor is to help people discern their wrongdoing and lead them in the way of repentance. We must therefore be able to distinguish between wrongdoing that is genuinely blocking a person's relationship with God, and temptations, weaknesses, limitations, and faults that may assume special importance because of an overscrupulous response. This capacity to distinguish righteousness from flawlessness is especially important when helping a person who has a problem with self-condemnation.

## Overcoming Self-Condemnation

What can we do to help people overcome a problem with self-condemnation, beyond merely dispelling the illusion that the problem is a virtue? I will offer here seven recommendations.

1. *Live righteously but avoid scrupulosity.* If a person does not want to *feel* guilty, the first step is not to *be* guilty. Objective guilt—wrongdoing—fuels a problem with self-condemnation

like gasoline flung on a raging fire. Unfortunately many pastors are tempted by secular therapies to help self-condemned people by bending basic standards of righteousness. This does a disservice to the individual and compromises the word of God. We should treat the self-condemned with special grace and compassion, but we should also exhort them to live a righteous life.

At the same time, we should help people lay aside overly scrupulous standards of conduct. Self-condemned people often take their weaknesses, limitations, and faults far too seriously. We will do them a great favor if we can help them consider their foibles and frailties with a healthy sense of humor. Christians should be earnest about living in righteousness but peaceful and patient in the face of weaknesses and limitations.

2. *Repair wrongdoing.* It is best simply to walk in righteousness, but all of us occasionally stumble and fall. We then must rise, slap the mud off our clothes, and walk on. We must repent, receive forgiveness, and press on to know the Lord.

As stated earlier, guilt is objective and can only be eliminated through objective means. When we sin against God and another human being, we do damage to a relationship that requires repair. Thus, repairing wrongdoing is a basic element in living a righteous life.

Repairing wrongdoing is also crucial for overcoming a problem with self-condemnation. Nothing provokes intense feelings of guilt as effectively as an accumulated burden of unresolved and unrepaired wrongdoing. Nothing soothes feelings of guilt as effectively as the assurance that one's wrongdoing is forgiven and a disrupted relationship is restored. It is therefore important that we teach people (especially those who have a problem with self-condemnation) how to repair damaged relationships.

I highly recommend an approach to repairing wrongdoing which incorporates these steps: A person who has committed wrongdoing (1) admits the wrongdoing; (2) renounces it (this step includes sorrow for sin); (3) asks forgiveness of the injured party; and (4) makes restitution. This approach applies both to our relationship with God and our relationships with brothers and sisters in Christ; it applies both to wrongs committed in the past and wrongs committed in the present. It is a simple, biblical method of restoring peace to broken relationships.[9]

This process of repairing wrongdoing can liberate an individual bound up by self-accusation and self-hatred. Of particular importance is the act of asking and receiving forgiveness. This act vividly conveys the healing knowledge that we have been released from the objective bondage of guilt and put at peace with God and man.

3. *Repent of Resentment.* Bitterness, resentment, and critical attitudes towards others are often only the flip side of one's negative attitudes toward oneself. The two sets of attitudes reinforce one another. It is therefore doubly important for people bound to self-condemnation to repent and turn aside from resentment and grudges that they hold against others—for the sake of perfect righteousness and also for the sake of perfect freedom.

Jesus said, "If you do not forgive men their trespasses, neither will your Father forgive your trespasses" (Mt 6:15). For the self-condemned it is also true to say, "If you do not forgive men their trespasses, neither will you be able to forgive your own trespasses."

4. *Distinguish useful from destructive guilt feelings.* We should not talk about guilt feelings as though they were always our enemies. Guilt feelings can fulfill a useful function, like physical pain, which often motivates us to care for a genuine physical need. Yet, as every athlete knows, the messages sent us by physical pain cannot always be taken seriously. Like athletes who quickly distinguish between a genuine problem and a passing sensation, Christians should be equipped to distinguish between guilt feelings that need to be taken seriously and those that need to be dismissed.

Positive and useful feelings of guilt have two characteristics: they reflect the presence of objective guilt, and they are expressed as contrition rather than as self-hatred. Destructive feelings of guilt, on the other hand, are irrational and condemning. They appear regardless of whether one has done right or wrong, and are thus not a reliable indicator of objective guilt; they are also expressed as self-condemnation and self-concern rather than as genuine godly grief. These guilt feelings should be resisted vigorously rather than welcomed hospitably. They cannot be relied on as a guide for the moral evaluation of conduct.

In many cases destructive guilt feelings are psychologically rooted in a person's experience of disapproval by others, especially those in authority. Such people have difficulty distinguishing guilt feelings from other people's disapproval of their actions. The pastor's goal is to help them make this distinction, so that they are free to do what is right even when others disagree.

People who habitually suffer from irrational, condemning feelings of guilt must acknowledge their emotional difficulty if any substantial change is to occur. It is not always easy to persuade someone that they have a problem in this area—they often prefer to see their guilt feelings as objective witnesses to their essential wickedness. Nonetheless, the problem cannot be defeated until it is recognized and actively resisted. The experience of a friend of mine illustrates this point.

He was persistently guilt-ridden. Every day he spent his time feeling bad about the 100 small things he thought he had done wrong. Much of his energy was eaten up by anxious thoughts over whether he had actually done something wrong. Though not perfect, he was basically a righteous young Christian man, earnest about following the Lord. Self-condemnation was choking his ability to move ahead.

My friend talked over his difficulty with one of his friends, someone who was more mature in Christian living and who could give him counsel. One day this man got angry with my friend. "Look," he said, "I'm sick and tired of hearing you say you're guilty when you aren't. I don't want to hear it any more. You shouldn't believe it any more. My advice to you is to decide not to feel guilty—to stop listening to your tyrannical conscience and the devil instead of the Holy Spirit. From now on, if you experience feelings of accusation, refuse to believe them; reject them unless you clearly discern that the charge is completely true. I know you want to follow the Lord. Let him show you what is wrong in your life, not the devil. The Lord will show you with simple clarity what you've done wrong and how to repair it. The devil wants to drag you down. Resist him."

My friend took this word to heart. As he made a determined response to guilt feelings and overscrupulous attitudes, he experienced a liberation from the difficulty. He learned that the action of the Holy Spirit in the heart of one who is earnestly seeking to follow the Lord brings light, peace, and joy and leads to change rather than continuing anguish.

Before moving on to the next point, it is worth noting that some people, rather than having difficulty distinguishing positive from destructive guilt, have the problem of not recognizing when they have done something wrong. They have too little positive guilt rather than too much of the destructive kind.

This is especially true of people who have been raised with a fluid approach to right and wrong, or who view themselves as wrong only if their intentions are bad, or who have lived for a long time as non-Christians. Such people may never have developed the proper instincts to cause them uneasiness about sexual misconduct, for example, or other kinds of wrongdoing. These people—and all of us to some degree—need to be sensitized to areas where their conscience is underdeveloped.

5. *Believe in God's forgiveness.* People with a self-condemnation problem commonly fail to accept the reality of God's forgiveness even after they have repented, confessed their sin, and asked for pardon. They cannot make significant progress in overcoming this problem until they receive in faith this fundamental Christian truth: *God forgives our sin when we come before him in repentance.*

John states this truth in the following manner: "If we confess our sins, he is faithful and just, and will forgive our sins and cleanse us from all unrighteousness" (1 Jn 1:9). Christian leaders need to proclaim and apply the doctrine of the forgiveness of sins in such a way that it ceases to be merely a theoretical truth for people and becomes instead an experienced reality.

6. *Seek help.* It might flatter our egos if we could work out all of our problems on our own, but God created us so that we need one another. In order to overcome a problem with self-condemnation, a Christian must usually look for help outside himself. To provide such individual, personalized assistance is part of a pastor's role. However, the pastor is not the only one who can do it. It is helpful if there are also other mature and wise Christians in the Christian body who can offer daily support and assistance to their brothers and sisters.

There are two main ways that those suffering under self-condemnation can seek help from others: through confessing wrongdoing and through seeking an outside judgment. A self-condemned Christian usually has failed to experience the fullness of God's forgiveness. Confessing wrongdoing to another person (one who is mature and wise) and receiving an assurance of God's forgiveness from a human mouth can provide immeasurable assistance. After all, scripture directs us to confess our sins to one another.

Seeking outside judgment is a way to overcome overscrupulousness. Another person can often see more clearly if wrongdoing has actually been committed, and if so how it should be dealt with. Thus, a pastoral advisor, either a full-time pastor or merely an experienced and mature Christian man or woman, can provide significant help for a person who has a problem with self-condemnation.

7. *Love one another.* One of the main sources of self-condemnation is poor relationships. Many people have grown up with emotional manipulation as a daily feature of life. People tend to exercise control over one another by showing emotional disapproval and withholding affection rather than by communicating their desires more directly. They also tend to nurse grudges and forgive with reluctance. This type of behavior fosters in many people a fear of others' emotional disapproval and a pervasive sense of being in the wrong.

Christians should relate differently than this. They should relate to one another directly and straightforwardly, without manipulation. They should forgive one another from the heart and effectively communicate this forgiveness through expressions of commitment and affection. Christians who relate to one another in love undo the damage of the past caused by defective relationships, and strengthen one another to serve the Lord in security and confidence. Our pastoring should aim to produce, by the grace of God, such relationships as this.

## Pastoral Emphases

In a society increasingly characterized by theoretical relativism and practical amorality, Christian pastoral leaders are obliged to emphasize the objectivity, solidity, and applicability of God's eternal law. However, in a society pervaded by anxiety, self-hatred, and emotional insecurity, we must also take care not to crush a bruised reed. People burdened by self-condemnation need wise counsel and warm encouragement, not just exhortations to obedience.

Thus the objectivity of guilt and the ideal of a clear conscience are complementary Christian truths of special importance. These truths should be taught side by side and effectively applied to people's lives. The Lord wants a righteous people who will serve him in freedom and confidence, unconstrained by the bonds of sin and self-condemnation.

# SIX

# What Should Christians Teach about Anger?

W HEN WE THINK OF ANGER, many manifestations come to mind, ranging from the cold shoulder to murder. The person who wakes up grumpy; the one who savors a grudge; the boss who regularly looses his cool; the neighbor who always makes caustic remarks; the depressed person who has capped a volcano of rage—all are experiencing anger.

When something goes wrong or does not go our way, a surge of emotion may rise in us. As our anger grows and our blood pressure mounts, we recognize a force within that has the power to dominate and the potential to consume both ourself and an adversary. If we lose control, our voice may become increasingly shrill until we find release in shouting; we may even come to blows with another.

## Anger as an Enemy

Anger is made up of both an inner reaction and the outward response. The two movements are so intertwined as to be virtually indistinguishable. But most of us have learned to recognize a point at which it is still possible to direct the force swelling mightily within so that it does not explode in violence without. Often we will decide not to express our anger out of fear that we will lose control. We tend to push it down; that is, we repress it. In fact, few people know how to use anger constructively. Hence, anger is commonly thought to be a bad, dangerous, or destructive emotion.

Many Christians take this negative view of anger and judge that it is always sinful. Anger out of control often poisons relationships, so there is plenty of firsthand evidence that it is an enemy to be avoided or subdued. Guilt feelings over angry outbursts reinforce this judgment.

What is more, Christians can cite selected scripture texts in support of this conclusion. In Galatians 5:20, Paul lists anger as a work of the flesh, along with sexual immorality, idolatry, envy, and other serious offenses. "But now," he writes to the Colossians, "put them all away: anger, wrath, malice, slander, and foul talk from your mouth" (3:8). He gives the same direction to the Ephesians (4:31).

Taken alone, these passages lead many Christians to the conclusion that anger is never right. Consequently, at the first hint of anger, out of fear or shame or conviction, they push the emotional reaction down, concluding that they have conquered and disarmed an enemy.

## The Selfist Approach

Another method of handling anger has gained enormous popularity in recent times. Secular counselors have redefined human nature, identifying *being* with *feeling*. Dr. David Viscott writes: "Living in our feelings, we are most in touch, most alive. To paraphrase Descartes, there is nothing more true than 'I feel, therefore, I am.' "[10]

Feelings, says this modern view, are givens—the fundamental personal realities that must be accepted. Happiness comes from following your feelings; if you attempt to control or change them, the result is misery. An increasing number of Christians in search of emotional wholeness have adopted this view, uncritically and contradictorily combining it with Christian teaching on the subject. Anger, described in this perspective as a powerful negative emotion, must be expressed openly.

Relief comes to the angry person only when the anger locates and redresses the original hurt.

Advice on how to handle anger this way varies, but always leads in the same direction: Be honest! Own up to your anger. Express it overtly. Confront the individual who hurt you. Tell it like it is. Make others aware of how you feel—don't let them wiggle out of it.

If for some reason confrontation is not possible, popular counselors prescribe other methods of letting anger out. Dr. Viscott, again:

> Imagine the person who has offended you dressed in ridiculous disguises, such as red tights and feathers. Or imagine him at a state banquet, nude and eating with his fingers. A ridiculous fantasy helps dissipate anger nicely and will put a smile on your face that will drive the other person absolutely crazy. Besides, the other person is already wearing a ridiculous disguise by being an angry person. Your fantasy will help you put that into perspective. . . .
>
> You can telephone the offending person keeping the button down, and let all your anger out. Anything that will put you in imaginary contact and release your feelings will work very nicely. Even if you feel silly, try it. . . .
>
> Pounding a pillow for 10 minutes also provides tremendous release . . . so does screaming. But be careful; these devices can become ends in themselves and should only be used as a substitute for the real thing when the actual person is unavailable or you haven't yet worked up the courage and ability to confront him directly.[11]

It must be said that there is some truth in the follow-your-feelings approach: Repression does not deal with anger effectively. A Christian ought to agree that repressing anger is wrong; it contradicts the biblical injunction to "*be* angry" (Eph 4:26).

However, the prescriptions of the follow-your-feelings movement are not true. The method does not work. "Letting anger out" indiscriminately does not resolve it. Like sexual desire, anger increases rather than decreases when indulged without discipline. Worse, the uncontrolled expression of anger contradicts scriptural teaching on anger: "Do not sin . . . give no opportunity to the devil" (Eph 4:26-27). Following the feeling of anger—letting it out of control or putting it in control—leads to grave emotional and spiritual problems. Among these are rage, resentment, hostility, broken relationships, and domination by evil spirits.

Both repression and uncontrolled expression of anger are unacceptable to a Christian. [12] If repression and undisciplined expression of anger are unacceptable to Christians, what is the right approach? It goes without saying that anger is a major source of difficulty for many in our congregations and groups. They must have Christian wisdom as well as grace to handle anger. So, what should pastors teach?

## *Our Human Makeup*

Correct use and handling of anger depends on a correct understanding. Christians must stop seeing anger negatively and must learn that it can be righteous.

God created anger for us and made it integral to our humanity. Along with other powerful emotions like fear and grief, he designed anger to be a valuable force in our life. It is a natural human reaction to obstacles. When we find ourselves in a frustrating situation, an angry reaction instinctively begins to work in us. God intends us to use this surge of emotion. It is meant to mobilize us for accomplishing things that demand effort and to equip us to fight through obstacles to what is right and good.

Anger is not wrong in itself. Getting angry is not necessarily a sin; it is sometimes righteous. Anger is righteous if it is directed against wrongdoing and is expressed in a controlled way. Anger is unrighteous if it is directed against something good; if it is allowed to get out of control or to control us; or if it expresses irritation at not getting our own way, hostility, or malice.

Christian teaching must clear away two obstacles to the understanding that anger is not intrinsically wrong and can be righteous. The first is a misreading of biblical teaching on anger. The second is a misconception that limits anger to its negative manifestations.

## The Scriptural View

Misinterpretation of the scriptural view of anger prevents many Christians from handling the emotion properly. Reference has already been made to some texts (Eph 4:31; Col 3:8; Gal 5:20) which, taken alone, lend support to the mistaken notion that anger is always wrong.

There are other passages, however, that make it clear that scripture teaches Christians to be cautious about anger, not to rule it out completely. "Be angry," Paul instructed the Ephesians (4:26), "but do not sin; do not let the sun go down on your anger, and give no opportunity to the devil." The passages in Proverbs 16:32 and James 1:19 warn us to be slow to anger, teaching us to govern its use, rather than to avoid it altogether.

The Lord Jesus himself gives a serious warning about anger, but he does not forbid it. "But I say to you that everyone who is angry with his brother *without cause* shall be liable to judgment" (Mt 5:22). "Without cause" is a qualifier present in ancient authoritative sources that verify the interpretation advanced here. The Lord is concerned about anger rooted in enmity and leading to murder. This brand of anger is always wrong. And even righteous anger must be expressed warily.

Thus, biblical teaching does not say that anger is always sinful. It prohibits anger out of control or in control of us (Prov 16:32; Jas 1:19), anger resulting in quarrels or dissension (Gal 5:20; Eph 4:26), and anger that is full of hatred or malice (Col 3:8; Eph 4:31; Mt 5:22). But within these biblical limits there is wide space for the righteous expression of anger.

Scriptural passages that describe the Lord's anger effectively dispel the misconception that anger is simply wrong. The Bible refers hundreds of times to the wrath of God. The gospels show us that Jesus got angry and directed his anger at people who were guilty of wrongdoing (Mt 23; Mk 3:5). The apostle Paul, who was scrupulously concerned to keep his conscience clear, got angry too. His letter to the Galatians is a good example of this kind of anger.

## Fruit of the Spirit

The second block to a correct understanding of anger is the commonly held misconception that restricts it to negative responses.

When they think of anger, most Christians have in mind overt negative manifestations like blowing up or quarreling. However, anger may be expressed constructively in various ways, such as through patience, steadfastness, and readiness to fight through an obstacle. All these could be identified as fruit of the Holy Spirit. To regard anger as a force contributing to the development of Christian character strikes a surprising note in most Christian circles. But it helps to present it to Christians in these terms.

Patience carries with it the notion of determination, as in the text, "Show the same earnestness in realizing the full assurance of hope until the end, so that you may not be sluggish, but imitators of those who through faith and patience inherit the promises" (Heb 6:11-12). When a Christian notices something wrong in himself or a situation he is responsible for, he can get angry and direct his anger into determination—a firm resolve to bring about a change.

Endurance or steadfastness is another channel for anger. I recall a university student who was enraged by a professor and classmates who mockingly challenged his Christian belief. Instead of displaying his anger directly, which though not unrighteous might have lost him some ground with his adversaries, he chose to stand firm in the face of their attacks. He may not have won arguments, but by his demeanor he won respect. His anger helped him handle himself well.

A third example of constructive expression of anger is aggressiveness. "Fight" is the word St. Paul chose to characterize the course of his Christian service (2 Tm 4:7).[13] Like anyone else, Christians encounter external obstacles in the form of inconveniences, delays, and confusion; and they come up against internal ones as well, such as temptation and distraction. Anger can help the Christian to deal with these problems aggressively. When a Christian encounters something wrong, he or she can get angry and fight through it, instead of becoming frustrated and depressed.

## Righteous Anger

While expanding our concept of anger to include determination, endurance, and aggressiveness, we should not rule out direct expressions of anger. At times it is right to communicate our anger to others. Speaking to someone about their wrongdoing, letting them know we are angry about it, can engage their will for repentance. A son who knows his father gets angry at dishonesty will think twice before telling a lie.

This does not constitute aquiescence to the follow-your-feelings approach. Speaking out in anger simply because we do not like something and are having a reaction is not appropriate Christian behavior. Nor is losing our temper or otherwise being out of control. Rather it is right—sometimes it may even be necessary—to openly express anger over sin, so long as we maintain control.

In fact, the main problem for Christians may be not too much anger, but too little. We do not get angry enough at the right objects. We tend to grow irritated over the little things that cross us rather than expressing anger at the sins of our society that merit the wrath of God and his servants. A pastor's goal should be to help Christians increase their experience of righteous anger and decrease the exercise of unrighteous anger.

## Three Practical Rules

Anger is supposed to be a useful emotion that supports a Christian in living righteously. For many it works in the opposite way, leading them into wrongdoing or depression. What wisdom is available to help a Christian handle anger properly? There is a sound, biblical strategy for handling anger in particular situations and for dealing with anger that has become an ongoing problem.

The strategy for handling anger in a particular situation is threefold: (1) do not repress anger; (2) express it righteously; and (3) settle things quickly. This pattern conforms to Paul's instruction to the Ephesians (4:26): (1) *be* angry; (2) do not sin; and (3) do not let the sun go down on your anger.

The first piece of advice is to not repress anger (be angry). Pushing it down does not deal with it. If anger can do a great deal of damage when released in a fit of temper, it can do equivalent or greater damage when repressed. The angry reaction does not dissipate but is expressed as cold anger and depression, internalized mirror images of hot anger and loss of control. While hot anger is no more or less righteous than cold anger, it is easier to deal with. The person who expresses his anger knows what he's dealing with and so does everyone around him. Repressed, indirectly expressed anger, however, is very hard to handle.

The repressed angry person falls into subtle wrongdoing: avoiding people, giving "the silent treatment," deliberately reneging on responsibilities, making negative wisecracks, indulging in self-pity. Often he does not realize that his actions are motivated by repressed anger. His immediate associates may be bewildered by his behavior: What is going on? Did someone do something wrong? Neither the angry person nor his associates are in a position to resolve the problem.

Unrighteous as it is, even losing one's temper at least offers the chance for immediate repentance and repair. Pushing anger down out of reach sets us up for unredressed wrongdoing.

The second piece of advice is to express anger righteously (do not sin). Anger does not have to be expressed in bursts of temper, nor does it have to impel us to do harm. When an angry reaction rises in us due to someone else's wrongdoing, we can address the problem, making the party involved aware of our anger. Or we can channel our anger constructively into determination to change things, endurance, forbearance, or readiness to fight past the obstacle. These expressions of anger have already been discussed.

Whatever ignited the angry reaction of anger, the expression must be in control if it is to be righteous. It is possible to communicate anger with great force and effect without losing one's temper. It is right to repent for anger out of control, but not for anger over wrongdoing, vigorously expressed but under control.

The last piece of advice is to settle things quickly (do not let the sun go down on your anger). Christians are well-advised to settle disputes and quarrels as quickly as possible. The sooner we deal with disruptions in our relationships the more easily will we be able to control and channel our anger.

## Problem Anger

Simply learning how to distinguish righteous from unrighteous anger will reduce the occurrence of the latter variety for many Christians. Learning to express anger righteously or channel it constructively can be experienced as an emancipation from emotional slavery.

Some people, however, will find only a little relief from receiving teaching along the lines I have presented. For numerous Christians anger is a sizable and persistent problem. Instruction about anger and even superhuman effort at constructively channeling it will not suffice to resolve their difficulty. They will still get angry regularly, for all the wrong reasons, and often their anger will veer out of control.

Dealing effectively with this kind of problem anger depends

on identifying its causes, of which there are four primary ones: (1) holding on to things, (2) resentment, (3) too much pressure, and (4) fears and inhibitions.

## Holding On

Sometimes we get angry because we are grasping something which we ought to be yielding to the Lord. When the same circumstances always trigger our anger, it is likely that we are holding on to something. We may want something badly and not be willing to let go. This can be obvious, as it is in anger over the death of a close relative or an unexpected pregnancy. Sometimes it is less obvious, like being unwilling to accept failure.

The solution is the same whether the root is obvious or not: surrender everything to the Lord. Teaching people to be thankful, no matter what, helps them yield all to the Lord. "Give thanks in all circumstances," Paul instructed the Thessalonians, "for this is the will of God in Christ Jesus for you" (1 Thes 5:18). Once they have surrendered everything to the Lord and are ready to thank him in all circumstances, people will be able to control their anger more easily and peacefully.

## Resentment

Resentment is another root to watch for in cases of uncontrollable anger. Resentment is a special form of anger that results from holding a grudge against a person who has hurt us in some way. Linked with it are more serious spiritual problems like hostility and malice. A resentful person desires to soothe his injury by injuring the offender. Resentment may damage its carrier more than the one against whom harm is intended, for it is a corrosive poison that destroys emotional health.

When we are injured we should forbear or forgive: "Put on then, as God's chosen ones . . . patience, forbearing one another and, if one has a complaint against another, forgiving each other; as the Lord has forgiven you, so you also must forgive"

(Col 3:12-13). Resentment sins against Christian love (1 Cor 13:5); revenge has no place in us, for vengence belongs to God alone (Rom 12:19). The Lord wants us to repent of resentment and put it away.

## Pressure

When we are under too much pressure we are more tense and more subject to anger, especially to that special form of anger called irritability. Pressure has many sources—overcommitment, deadlines, mental and emotional overwork, trying too hard, perfectionism. For the problem of constant irritability, the solution often is to let up and relax in some area of our lives. A person may have to review his priorities and set some aside or accept a lower standard of achievement for himself and those around him. He may have to be satisfied with good rather than best; but it will be better for him to be thus rid of irritability.

## Fears and Inhibitions

Persistent anger is sometimes a symptom of other emotional problems. Fears and inhibitions, for example, are roots of anger because they prevent a person from acting confidently and decisively. The resulting frustration is a form of anger that we more often than not feel toward others rather than ourselves. When anger is the byproduct of other emotional disorders, its correction depends on theirs. The cure for fearfulness and inhibition comes in large measure from the determination to serve others ahead of ourselves and from the formation of solid Christian personal relationships.

In fact, the key to emotional wholeness—the secret to freedom from control by powerful emotions like anger—lies in placing preeminent concern on conducting our personal relationships righteously and making sure that our feelings support us in the effort.

# SEVEN

# The Gift of Fear

THE PASTORAL LEADER WHO DECIDES to instruct his congregation or group in the Christian approach to fear will have to work hard to persuade people that fear can be anything but bad. It is easy for all of us to recognize more pleasant emotions—attraction, delight, enthusiasm, joy—as gifts. But many folks, if they were to hear that the Lord gave them fear as a gift, would look for the customer service counter to exchange it for something more to their liking.

Yet the Lord has assigned fear a constructive purpose in our lives. In fact, there are various kinds of fear, with various purposes.

For example, consider the kind of fear that equips us to respond quickly to danger. It comes into play automatically when we must be motivated to deal with a threat. When we see a fire out of control, fear is our instinctive reaction. Sufficiently alerted, we are ready to respond properly and effectively by attempting to put out the fire or by sounding the alarm and exiting, whichever prudence dictates. This kind of fear is an internal activation system designed to save our lives, a God-given safety mechanism of the highest importance.

Other kinds of fear—cautiousness, timidity, reserve, and so on—are character traits and states of mind rather than instantaneous emotional responses. These may be good or bad. Finally, there is fear which is a matter of deliberate expression. For instance, scripture tells us to "fear God" or "fear the emperor." Obviously, this too can be a good kind of fear.

Are the various kinds of fear good or bad? Clearly it depends on whether the behavior which results is right or wrong, helpful or harmful. Fear as an emotional reaction, like other emotional reactions such as anger and guilt, is itself morally neutral. What determines whether it is good or bad is our response to it. The same is true of the other types of fear. Recognizing this opens the way for an examination of some types of fear, and this will lead us naturally to consider how to teach Christians about fear and how to help them deal with problems in this area.

## *The Beginning of Wisdom*

Scripture places a high value on the fear of the Lord, which it says is "the beginning of wisdom." However, many modern Christian recoil at the thought of fearing God. Some have reached the conclusion that God is too kind to punish men and women for their wrongdoing, and so there is no reason to fear him. Others have embraced the notion that if a person fears God he or she could never really love him.

Some support for this view seems to come from the familiar statement in John's first letter that "perfect love casts out fear." In other words, God's perfect love for us displaces our fear of him. Jesus' words to Peter when he fell at his knees and begged him to depart were, "Do not be afraid."

But clearly the message of these passages cannot be that fear of God has no place in the Christian life. Mary sings that "his mercy is on those who fear him"; Luke tells us that the early church was built up "walking in the fear of the Lord and in the comfort of the Holy Spirit"; Paul writes about making "holiness perfect in the fear of God."

The kind of fear of God which the gospel takes away is the dread of punishment, the conviction that as a sinful being one is destined for God's wrath (see 1 Jn 4:17-18). The fear which is both the "beginning of wisdom" and the "perfecting of holiness" (2 Cor 7:1) is a realistic response to God's overwhelming greatness and righteousness. This sort of fear is not incompatible with love for God but goes hand in hand with it. In fact, only when we come to know the Lord as he is and to acquire a healthy fear of him are we in a position to love him correctly.

"This is the love of God," John wrote in his first letter, "that we keep his commandments" (1 Jn 5:3). Fear of the Lord leads us to obey him, which is to love him. God's demand for obedience is, likewise, an expression of his love for us. It is loving of God to warn us that it is simply dangerous for humans to disregard who he is and to disobey him.

When scripture counsels us to fear God, it is speaking more of the ways we act toward God than of the feelings we have about him. Fear of God may have an emotional component. The crowds who followed Jesus were awed by the miracles he worked. Sometimes we are struck with a sense of holy fear at God's majesty. But when scripture tells us to fear God, it is not instructing us to stir up feelings of awe, which we can hardly do on our own, but to order our thoughts and conduct conscious of God's supreme power and holiness.

## Reverence and Respect

We sometimes fail to recognize references to fear in scripture because the terms for it are often translated in ways that do not immediately bring fear to mind. Thus Paul's instructions regarding household relationships in Ephesians 5:21 are sometimes rendered, "Be subject to one another out of reverence for Christ." "Reverence" here is the translation of the Greek word for fear, *phobos.* The point of the passage is that we ought to relate to one another in definite ways, and that this behavior is motivated by a proper fear of Christ, an authority we cannot ignore.

Reverence in this biblical sense means acting carefully and respectfully when we come before a worthy person or object. It means fearful behavior, not of the running away or timid variety but of the sort that is a response to one who has power, one whom we cannot disregard without serious consequences.

"Respect" is another word that conceals the term for fear. In Romans 13:7, "Pay all of them their dues . . . respect to whom respect is due," and 1 Peter 2:18, "Servants, be submissive to your masters with all respect," respect is the word used to translate the same Greek word for fear, *phobos*. In these contexts showing respect means behaving in ways that indicate proper regard for people who have authority.

Fear of the Lord, reverence, and respect are good if they are directed in the right way, wrong if they are not. It is right to fear God, wrong to revere Hindu deities. It is right to respect our parents, wrong to revere evil spirits.

## Caution and Cowardice

Other forms of fear are good or bad depending on the circumstances. Traits such as cautiousness, carefulness, and conservatism, which contain a kernel of fear, are neutral qualities that must be evaluated according to whether they help us do what we should.

A cautious person is one who does not act until he or she is fairly sure that it is safe to do so. It would be good to be cautious when walking through a mine field. But it is not good to approach every situation with a great deal of caution. Excessive caution can prevent us from doing things the Lord calls us to do which involve some dangers.

Conservatism is a wariness of change. A conservative approach may be either good or bad. Sometimes conservatism is useful because it holds on to something which is worthwhile; it may even prevent disaster. But at other times it may be an obstacle to valuable changes.

Timidity and cowardice are also words that refer to forms of fear. A timid person is one who always holds back; a coward is someone who gives in to fear and is not willing to do what he must. Timidity and cowardice are close in meaning and are varieties of fear that are always bad.

## Social Fears and Anxiety

Nothing has been said yet about a predominant expression of fear in our society—social fears. Pastoral leaders who want to teach their people about dealing with fear should recognize that the main form which afflicts people today is social fear, that is, fears which arise in personal relationships.

When the Bible discusses fear, it normally refers to concrete dangers—invaders, battles, famine, plague. For contemporary Christians fear has more to do with losing social approval. This is not to say that we do not experience fear of danger or that people in biblical times did not experience social fears. However, the fear of being disliked and rejected by others is much more prominent now than it was in the past.

Fears of loneliness, rejection, and disapproval are expressed in a constellation of behavior patterns. Among these are reserve and shyness (the tendency to be closed to others or the inability to be expressive in relationships), timidity, dishonesty (in the sense of concealing ourselves behind facades), and personal insecurities. As pastoral leaders we must develop a strategy that can help people deal with these widespread social fears.

Finally, we must say a word about anxiety. Anxiety is sometimes understood to refer to worry about particular things. For example, many people are excessively concerned about their bodies, their health. We all know people who are anxious about disease or weight. Some people are anxious about harm coming to loved ones, or about their personal relationships falling apart (especially when they are based more on emotional dependence than real commitment). Anxiety may also refer to worry about everything in general. People sometimes find themselves devoured by a gnawing fear that nothing will work out right.

## The Christian Approach to Fear

The Lord does not want his people to be paralyzed by fears of any kind. In his design for us fear ought to serve us by evoking right responses: reverence for the Lord, respect for authority, fear of mortal dangers. He does not want fear to immobilize his servants, preventing them from doing what is right.

Pastoral leaders can do a lot to help their people deal with fear in a proper Christian way. Teaching about the different kinds of fear described above is in itself a great benefit. Learning that fear is often helpful is good news to those who have believed that fear is always destructive.

What further teaching can pastoral leaders offer and what strategies and approaches can they employ to aid people in dealing with fear so that it functions as their servant rather than their enemy or master?

Our goal is to prepare people to handle fear as the Lord intended them to. The aim of the Christian life is the transformation of men and women into the image and likeness of Jesus Christ. We must desire that people grow in godly character so that they habitually and instinctively respond in situations as the Lord himself would.

## Confidence

Two character traits sum up the right Christian behavior in the face of fear: confidence and courage. Our lives should not be characterized by timidity, cowardice, excessive conservatism, anxiety, or social fears. The Lord wants us to become confident and courageous in our response to the situations we find ourselves in. These traits are fruit of the Holy Spirit because they are qualities produced in us by the Spirit as marks of our adopted sonship.

This confidence has more to do with overcoming the fears that derive from social situations than with those triggered by objective dangers. A Christian man or woman may be convinced that he or she cannot relate well to others, and so distance themselves in fear, being closed, unexpressive, and indirect. A confident Christian, however, will be open, expressive, decisive, and straightforward in personal relationships. Christians must learn that, by grace, confidence can drive away their social insecurities.

Sam is a case in point. For the most part he was living an effective Christian life. One of Sam's prominent weaknesses, however, was his tendency to withdraw in social settings.

I explained to him that the Lord wanted him to be able to relate to people openly, speaking up when he had something to say and refusing to hide in the crowd. I encouraged him to contribute more actively to dinner conversations at home, even if he thought what he had to say was unimportant or uninteresting.

Later, he was asked to take on Christian service that required him to greet large numbers of people he had never met before. Over a considerable period of time, he found himself having to take the lead in conversations with groups of people, something which he learned to do well. Little by little, Sam found that confidence was replacing his timidity. Now he no longer has trouble with his former insecurities.

## *Courage*

Courage, or boldness, is another correct Christian response to fear. To respond to a situation with courage does not mean to be without fear. A courageous person is willing to act with strength despite feelings of fear. He or she is one who is not scared off by dangers.

When the Lord commissioned Joshua to take the promised land from enemies who were apparently stronger than the Israelites, he gave him this instruction: "Be strong and of good courage, do not fear or be in dread of them: for it is the Lord your God who goes with you; he will not fail you or forsake you" (Dt 31:6). The people of Israel were facing a very real danger, but the Lord wanted them to be courageous. By not running away from a strong enemy they would give the Lord an opportunity to act on their behalf. The same principle applies to Christians.

A Christian must be courageous especially when encountering danger in the course of accomplishing some task that the Lord wants to be done. When the chief priests and elders tried to prevent the apostles from preaching and healing in the name of Jesus, the Christians prayed for courage to speak the word, and the Lord granted their prayer by the power of the Holy Spirit: "And when they had prayed, the place in which they were gathered together was shaken; and they were all filled with the Holy Spirit and spoke the word of God with boldness" (Acts 4:31). When opponents attempted to block the work of Christ by thrusting Paul into jail, others grew bold and continued the task. Paul writes that "most of the brethren have been made confident in the Lord because of my imprisonment, and are much more bold to speak the word of God without fear" (Phil 1:14).

However, what sometimes looks like boldness is actually foolhardiness. To distinguish boldness from folly, or prudence from cowardice, we must rely on the wisdom that comes from our Christian experience. No set of guidelines exists that will simplify the process. When we know that it is right to do something, we should do it regardless of fear. But we must learn how to draw upon the wisdom we receive from the Holy Spirit and from our common sense. It is one thing to win the crown of martyrdom for our fidelity and quite another to be martyred because of our stupidity.

Teaching people that they should grow in confidence and courage and expecting them to manifest this fruit of the Holy Spirit is fundamental to their ability to master fear.

## Antidotes for Fear

Faith and fight are antidotes to fear. They are elements of the Lord's strategy for bringing fear into a position of service in our lives.

Faith in the Lord overcomes fear of objective dangers and enemies as well as social fears and worries. This truth is plainly declared in the Old Testament, especially in the Psalms. "Even though I walk through the valley of the shadow of death, I fear no evil; for thou art with me; thy rod and thy staff, they comfort me" (Ps 23:4). "The Lord is my light and my salvation; whom shall I fear? The Lord is the stronghold of my life; of whom shall I be afraid? When evildoers assail me . . . they shall stumble and fall. Though a host encamp against me, my heart shall not fear" (Ps 27:1-3).

The New Testament is even stronger on this point: not only is faith the antidote for fear, it is simply wrong for a Christian to be fearful or anxious.

And he said to his disciples, "Therefore I tell you, do not be anxious about your life, what you shall eat, nor about your body, what you shall put on. For life is more than food, and the body more than clothing. Consider the ravens: they neither sow nor reap, they have neither storehouse nor barn, and yet God feeds them. Of how much more value are you than the birds! And which of you by being anxious can add a cubit to his span of life? If then you are not able to do as small a thing as that, why are you anxious about the rest? . . . And do not seek what you are to eat and what you are to drink, nor be of anxious mind. For all the nations of the world seek these things; and your Father knows that you need them. Instead, seek his kingdom, and these things shall be yours as well."
(Lk 12:22-26, 29-32)

The Lord's commands in this passage boil down to this: stop being anxious and have faith (see also Lk 12:4-5 and 1 Pt 5:7). Practically speaking, faith as an antidote to fear means that people must take advantage of all the spiritual resources the Lord has given them. As pastoral leaders teach their people that faith overcomes fear, they must also help them grow in their relationship to God. This means being sure that Christians are expressing their love for the Lord by making use of the normal means of Christian growth, especially daily prayer and study of scripture. Pastors who want to train Christians to be free of problems with fear will train them to fear the Lord. Every

Christian must simply put God first and do everything necessary to build a relationship with him. If people do not maintain close contact with the Lord, they will be distancing themselves from the only one who can deliver them from their fears.

Having faith also means letting the Holy Spirit work to release us from fear's bondage. Yielding an area of our life to the Holy Spirit means allowing him to change us within so that we can conform our behavior more exactly to God's ways. The teaching of scripture is that a Christian can overcome timidity by engaging the power of the Holy Spirit. "I remind you to rekindle the gift of God that is within you through the laying on of my hands; for God did not give us a spirit of timidity but a spirit of power and love and self-control" (2 Tm 1:6-7). Any Christian as a part of his prayer time or on the spot in the face of some fear can call on the Holy Spirit to make him bold.

## Special Prayer for Problem Fear

A pastoral leader may want to provide an opportunity for individuals to receive special prayer if they seem to have more than the usual difficulty with fear. This kind of prayer is sometimes called prayer for inner healing and includes deliverance from evil spirits. The leader and one or two others might meet with the person to counsel him and to pray particularly for release in the area of fear.

In this kind of ministry we are asking the Holy Spirit to focus his power directly on the fear. In such cases, we are seeking an outpouring of grace that will enable the individual to deal more effectively with fear when he or she experiences it again.

Prayer for inner healing and deliverance work best when the pastoral leader has a continuing personal relationship with the individual. Special prayer sessions are valuable because the Lord can be counted on to work powerfully in people's lives when we ask him to. But how a person conducts himself in the days after prayer for inner healing and deliverance is more important than the session itself. The proof of the pudding is in the eating. The test of inner healing and deliverance from fear is whether the person grows in courage day by day and acts accordingly. [14]

## Fighting Fear

Christians who want to be free from fear must take an active and responsible approach to their fears. They must even be aggressive in putting fears in their place or in warding them off. Thus, fight is the second element in our strategy. Fight means refusing to let feelings of fear determine our actions. When we are afraid in the face of something we must do, fight enables us to accomplish the deed in spite of our internal state.

Several years ago, when I was involved in ministry to university students, I was asked to give a presentation to a gathering of their parents. Some of my colleagues had prepared an outline for the presentation, based on their experience with similar meetings. The speaker was supposed to both encourage the parents and to correct them for refusing to forgive their children for past injuries.

As I surveyed the roomful of men and women, all of whom were about twenty years my senior, I was struck with fear. "Why should I have to give this talk? These folks will say I'm wet behind the ears. Who am I to be advising them? One of the guys who dreamed up this talk should be giving it!"

I remember deciding to drive these thoughts from my mind. I reminded myself that the teaching I was about to give was simply an application of God's word and that these good people would appreciate hearing it. As I began to speak, the feelings of fear left. I delivered the presentation confidently and, I think, effectively.

The mental discipline I employed to ward off fear was a form of fight. Disciplining our thoughts is one of the main ways of replacing timidity with courage, insecurity with confidence. We should teach people to recognize that streams of negative thoughts may flood them with fears. They should be trained to choke off the streams at their source and to replace them with a true and accurate perspective.

The Christian perspective always includes the power of the Holy Spirit. The mental discipline that cuts fear down to size is rooted in grace. Fight that attempts to handle fear on its own strength is inadequate. Fight that draws its clout from the Spirit of the One who raised Jesus Christ from death has real power to overcome fear's paralyzing effects.

## Rationalizing Fears—An Obstacle

One obstacle to fighting fear is our tendency to rationalize fearfulness into an acceptable feature of our personality. People make themselves comfortable with fear: "Well, I'm just a shy person." I have known Christians who praised the "humility" of a brother so fear-ridden that he hardly ever spoke to others. Insecurity sometimes causes people to talk aimlessly and too much; they describe themselves as "outgoing." Anxiety too is often approached as though it were a condition that just comes over us, a state of being which we can do nothing about.

Rationalization causes fears to cling closely to us. Fearfulness becomes an unquestionable part of us—a quirk, a trait, a condition, even a virtue. Such improper thinking puts fear in control and out of the reach of any efforts to fight it.

We should teach people to admit that what is wrong is *wrong*. We should train them to make a problem unwelcome by identifying it by its accurate, unattractive name. For instance, when a person always hangs back, teach him to describe his state as cowardice not prudence. We should not allow people to hang on to timidity and anxiety as though these are either valuable or unchangeable traits. These are problems and should be dealt with as such. The Lord loves to correct such problems, for he wants a people who are courageous and unafraid.

## Practical Pointers

As we gain experience in our efforts to help people implement this strategy, we will accumulate a body of practical advice. The following practical pointers have been tried and found effective.

First, accept suffering. A Christian leader who wants his congregation or group to handle fear with greater freedom must help them to accept the place of suffering in their lives. Living the Christian life does not mean that everything will work right. Often it does not, and sometimes it hurts. Once people are willing to endure suffering, fear will be much less of a difficulty for them (see 1 Pt 3:13-17).

Peter declared this truth in his first letter:

> Now who is there to harm you if you are zealous for what is right? But even if you do suffer for righteousness' sake, you will be blessed. Have no fear of them, nor be troubled, but in your hearts reverence Christ as Lord. Always be prepared to make a defense to anyone who calls you to account for the hope that is in you, yet do it with gentleness and reverence; and keep your conscience clear, so that, when you are abused, those who revile your good behavior in Christ may be put to shame. For it is better to suffer for doing right, if that should be God's will, than for doing wrong. (1 Pt 3:13-17)

Christians who are ready to suffer have a lot less to be afraid of. They will place their confidence in the Lord and expect that he will bring good out of their hurt.

Second, face the fear. An aggressive approach to fighting fear involves helping people face up to fearful situations. We can decide to encourage people under our pastoral care to do the things they are afraid of.

A few months ago Ted, a young businessman, was assigned by his boss to address a group of foremen on the topic of goal setting. Unaccustomed as Ted was to public speaking—let alone instructing a group of men, each of whom was old enough to be his father—he became very anxious. He began to worry about the presentation, devoting an inordinate number of hours to preparing for it.

When I saw that Ted was letting fear dominate this situation, I spoke to him about it. I asked him to review with me his plans for the presentation. After looking over the materials and even hearing him give part of the talk, I was able to assure him that he would do a very good job. I asked him to limit his preparation time to three more hours (he was planning on fifteen). I all but commanded him to stop worrying about it.

My assurance that he would do well helped Ted to face the situation. He did so well that two high executives in his large company of 6000 employees sought him out to congratulate him on a fine job. Any more successes like this one and I will have to sit Ted down to talk to him about pride.

Third, work gradually. Sometimes people make progress against fear when they chip away at it little by little. A person who suffers from insecurity may be able to become self-confident by piling up a series of small victories. One who is anxious about many things can begin to contain the problem by working on one area at a time. Having ceased to worry about how her children are going to turn out, a single parent can then work at not being anxious about money. Sometimes faith moves mountains by dislodging them and casting them into the sea. Faith can also move a mountain shovel by shovel.

Fourth, put someone in charge. People may be able to learn to have faith and fight if someone else takes a directive role in training them to deal with fear. The pastoral leader or another Christian friend could be made responsible for a definite period of time to lead a person out of fear. This approach adds up to giving a counselor the authority to apply the strategy for overcoming fear. The adviser teaches, encourages, holds the person steady in the face of a fearful situation, decides what to work on next, and so on. The stories above about Sam and Ted illustrate this point.

Fifth, discourage introspection. Anxious thoughts tend to encourage introspection. People easily become preoccupied with things they worry about. One of the ways that fear immobilizes people is to turn them in on themselves. Pastoral leaders should teach people to resist being introspective. This does not mean that we should discourage people from understanding their emotions. But Christians must resist the temptation to be absorbed by emotions like fear.

In addition to resisting tendencies to introspection, people must have opportunities to speak to others about their difficulties. Pastoral leaders should work at developing ways for people in their congregations and groups to talk with other members about their lives, including their fears.

Sixth, deal with external factors. Sometimes fear is generated by external factors. Anxiety, for example, is sometimes caused by too much pressure or too many commitments. If this is the case, the external situation must be changed before the internal reaction can be dealt with. Having an orderly schedule, with commitments cut back to reasonable proportions, may bring enough peace to a person's life for them to conquer fear. In fact, correction of external factors alone can sometimes eliminate the problem a person is having.

Seventh, build relationships. Pastoral leaders who decide to help their people with fear and other emotional problems must pay attention to personal relationships in their groups. Social fears are byproducts of bad relationships. A prevailing negativity, the failure to keep commitments, the absence of encouragement and affection all conspire to cause insecurity in people. Anxiety, too, can be generated by bad relationships. A wife may be overwhelmed with worry that is rooted in her husband's irresponsibility. Pastoral care that supports sound relationships is essential for the emotional health of the people in our care.

Helping people get free from emotional problems is worth the effort. A congregation or group full of strong and confident men and women who use their emotions as resources will do a lot more of the Lord's work a lot more effectively. Investing time and energy in the emotional health of God's people brings a great return.

# Notes

1. George A. Butterick, ed., *Interpreter's Dictionary of the Bible* (Nashville: Abingdon Press, 1962) 2:1000.
2. *Ibid.*
3. John L. McKenzie, *Dictionary of the Bible* (Riverside, New Jersey: Macmillan, 1965), p. 591.
4. Gustav Stahlin, *orge,* in Gerhard Friedrich, ed. *Theological Dictionary of the New Testament* (Grand Rapids, Michigan: Eerdmans, 1967) 5:424-25.
5. J. Pedersen, *Israel* (Oxford: Oxford University Press, 1926) 1:127-28.
6. *Ibid.,* p. 132.
7. David Viscott, *The Language of Feelings* (New York: Pocket Books, 1977), p. 22.
8. Harry E. Gunn, *Manipulation by Guilt* (Waukegan, Illinois: Great Lakes Living Press, Ltd., 1978), p. 6.
9. See Ken Wilson's *How to Repair the Wrong You've Done* (Ann Arbor, Michigan: Servant Books, 1981) for a detailed description of this process.
10. Viscott, p. 13.
11. *Ibid.,* pp. 103-104.
12. For further discussion on these points see Jay E. Adam's excellent commentary in *The Christian Counselor's Manual* (Grand Rapids, Michigan: Baker Book House), pp. 348-53 and notes.
13. See Peter Williamson's "Will the Assertive Inherit the Earth?" *Pastoral Renewal,* vol. 4, no. 2 (August 1979), for a description of the place of aggressive behavior in the Christian life.
14. Before a church or Christian group decides to initiate this type of ministry, I recommend that the leaders study Michael Scanlan's and Randall Cirner's fine book, *Deliverance from Evil Spirits* (Ann Arbor, Michigan: Servant Books, 1981). While these men write from their experience as Roman Catholics, their pastoral wisdom applies to all Christians.

# Suggested Reading

Applewhite, Barry. *Feeling Good about Your Feelings* (Wheaton, Illinois: Victor Books, 1980).

A pastor looks at what scripture has to say about the emotions. Written for the lay person, the book covers such topics as anger, sorrow, joy, anxiety, fear, love, compassion, and loneliness.

Baars, Conrad W. *Feeling and Healing Your Emotions* (Plainfield, New Jersey: Logos International, 1979).

A clinical psychologist offers a Christian perspective geared for the nonprofessional. Written in a question-and-answer format, the book offers advice for coping with and channeling negative feelings and for giving positive ones a healthier climate in which to thrive.

Backus, William, and Chapian, Marie. *Telling Yourself the Truth* (Minneapolis: Bethany Fellowship, 1980).

A psychologist and psychotherapist team up to present a Christian approach to the emotions. They point out that how we think determines how we feel. Through what they call "misbelief therapy," they present an approach for people who want to learn to control their emotions.

Cirner, Therese. *The Facts about Your Feelings* (Ann Arbor, Michigan: Servant Books, 1982).

Cirner has written a lifelong resource book for women of every age and background, which is excellent for both personal use and for use by small groups.

Ghezzi, Bert. *The Angry Christian* (Ann Arbor, Michigan: Servant Books, 1980).

The author maintains that most Christians don't get angry often enough. He offers ample illustrations and sound advice, based on scripture and pastoral experience, to help Christians handle anger in the right way.

Kinzer, Mark. *Living with a Clear Conscience* (Ann Arbor, Michigan: Servant Books, 1982).

Kinzer distinguishes between genuine guilt and emotional problems masquerading as guilt and offers a practical strategy for overcoming guilt and self-condemnation.

Kinzer, Mark. *The Self-Image of a Christian* (Ann Arbor, Michigan: Servant Books, 1980).

The author offers help for overcoming the problems connected with a false self-image, such as insecurity, self-doubt, timidity, and discouragement.

Strauss, Richard L. *Win the Battle for Your Mind* (Wheaton, Illinois: Victor Books, 1980).

Strauss offers a biblical approach that aims to help Christians resist the forces that try to influence the way they think. He presents practical advice for the person who wants to learn to control and train his mind.

Vitz, Paul C. *Psychology as Religion: The Cult of Self-Worship* (Grand Rapids, Michigan: William B. Eerdmans, 1977).

A professor of psychology at New York University offers an insightful critique of modern psychology. Vitz argues convincingly that selfist psychology has become part of the problem of modern life rather than part of its resolution. He concludes that psychology has become a religion, a form of secular humanism based on worship of the self.